D0456977

God in the Flesh

What Speechless Lawyers, Kneeling Soldiers and
Shocked Crowds Teach Us About Jesus

Don Everts

InterVarsity Press
Downers Grove, Illinois

InterVarsity Press
P.O. Box 1400, Downers Grove, IL 60515-1426
World Wide Web: www.ivpress.com
E-mail: mail@ivpress.com

©2005 by Don Everts

All rights reserved. No part of this book may be reproduced in any form without written permission from InterVarsity Press.

InterVarsity Press® is the book-publishing division of InterVarsity Christian Fellowship/USA®, a student movement active on campus at hundreds of universities, colleges and schools of nursing in the United States of America, and a member movement of the International Fellowship of Evangelical Students. For information about local and regional activities, write Public Relations Dept., InterVarsity Christian Fellowship/USA, 6400 Schroeder Rd., P.O. Box 7895, Madison, WI 53707-7895, or visit the IVCF website at <www.intervarsity.org>.

Scripture quotations, unless otherwise noted, are from the New Revised Standard Version of the Bible, copyright 1989 by the Division of Christian Education of the National Council of the Churches of Christ in the USA. Used by permission. All rights reserved.

Design: Matt Smith

Images: Creatas

ISBN 0-8308-3287-4

Printed in the United States of America ∞

Library of Congress Cataloging-in-Publication Data

Everts, Don, 1971-
  God in the flesh: what speechless lawyers, kneeling soldiers, and
  shocked crowds teach us about Jesus/Don Everts.
    p. cm.
  Includes bibliographical references.
  ISBN 0-8308-3287-4 (cloth: alk. paper)
  1. Incarnation. 2. Bible. N.T. Gospels—Criticism, interpretation,
  etc. I. Title.
  BT220.E94 2005
  232.9—dc22

                                                              2005005130

P	18	17	16	15	14	13	12	11	10	9	8	7	6	5	4	3	2	1
Y	19	18	17	16	15	14	13	12	11	10	09	08	07	06	05			

I decided to know nothing among you except Jesus Christ, and him crucified.

1 Corinthians 2:2

Contents

Introduction

How I Tried Not to Write This Book and Failed

I tried not to write this book. I really did.

In a world where we are inundated with tens of thousands of new titles a year, a world where anyone who can write does, where our shelves are already near to full with centuries' worth of excellent books about Jesus—I took a great pause before presuming to bother our world's perfectly fine trees with another title to die for.

I failed, obviously. And wrote. We'll see if it was the right move. May God grant me mercy for this decision. And may he grant you mercy as you bother to break the spine on yet another book.

And why did I fail, you may wonder? I failed because Jesus is just so beautiful. And the enemy is just such a liar.

Jesus has always been beautiful. He is, after all, the image of the invisible God. God in the flesh. And seeing him clearly, staring at him and all that his life and death reveal, changes us. That's what the church has always been—simple folks who stare at Jesus and are changed because of what they've seen.

That's why our enemy lies about Jesus and celebrates when

our clear picture of Jesus becomes a little less clear. The enemy has always been that way. And in every age he fumbles around with new lies, subtle new deceptions to keep the church from seeing the flesh of God revealed in Jesus and being changed.

And so I wrote.

I wrote because Jesus is God in the flesh. And that is a miracle too amazing to treat casually—we should be staring at Jesus with a relentless and joyful zeal.

I wrote because it is essential that we remain centered upon Jesus, that we see him clearly and not allow the enemy to blur our vision of him. I wrote because the Gospels are so theologically adequate and yet so seldom seriously studied, because they are so full of details about Jesus that we tend to overlook.

I wrote because I honestly believe that many of the problems we face (both individually and corporately) stem from our lack of focus on Jesus. And because our image of Jesus has grown blurry and smudged from neglect.

I wrote because the enemy hates clarity and has been having his way with our image of Jesus. He's pleased with himself. And I have grown tired of his swagger.

In the end, I wrote because the act of writing causes me to stare more intently at Jesus. And that is a grace. I wrote because I am tired and because staring at Jesus refreshes me.

And what I've written is a book about Jesus. It's a celebration of his life and of everything that is revealed in him and made clear in him. It is, ultimately, an intent look at the very flesh of God.

In the first two chapters we'll consider the place that Jesus had in the life of the early church and why our image of him today gets blurred so easily. These chapters are foundational, explaining the need for this book and the posture of the chapters that follow. Chapters three through ten are the book proper, the true meat of this study. They are written to help us see Jesus more clearly.

In them we'll study some simple verses from the forgotten corners of the Gospels, allowing our vision of Jesus to come into greater focus.

These little verses we'll be studying may seem boring at first glance, but they have come to thrill me over time. They have taught me more about Jesus' life and presence and authority and compassion and call than I ever thought possible. The Gospels are indeed rich. Even seemingly insignificant, often neglected verses from the Gospels are dripping with theology and truth and clarity about Jesus.

I pray that looking at these verses will be as surprising and shocking and refreshing for you as it has been for me. May God bless you as you stare at his very flesh.

Book One
The Life of Jesus

The early church was a Jesus-consumed group of people. Their conversations and letters and sermons and songs were saturated with his name. Their communities were preoccupied with the simple stories of his life.

Why were they so centered on Jesus? And what can we learn from their attentiveness to his life?

Chapter One
Fixing Our Eyes on Jesus

No one has ever seen God.

Let's just start right there. God is invisible. We've all cursed that fact, railed against it, shook our fists at the heavens in the general direction (so we think) of this frustratingly invisible God. But so it is.

Out God is invisible.

But despite his invisibility, we know that God longs to be known. Throughout the centuries he has gone to great pains to reveal himself—in visions, images, angelic visits, dreams, soft winds, thick clouds, burning bushes, columns of smoke, a donkey and, of course, audible speech. His sheer creativity in revealing himself shows us just how much he longs to be known.

And this great longing in God had its ultimate culmination in a seemingly small event.

A baby was born. The baby cried and had rashes and spit up and giggled and learned to walk. But this fleshy baby had something in it other than milk and cries and soft coos: all of the fullness of the invisible God dwelt within that soft skin.

God had unleashed his Fleshy Baby Plan in a small, out-of-the-way town and was about to reveal himself to an extent no one could have imagined.

The opening sentence of the epistle to the Hebrews begins by pointing out this thrilling historic shift: "Long ago God spoke to our ancestors in many and various ways by the prophets, but in these last days he has spoken to us by a Son" (Hebrews 1:1-2).

At the beginning of his Gospel, John writes simply and beautifully of God's strategy, "No one has ever seen God. [Thanks for rubbing it in, John!] It is God the only Son, who is close to the Father's heart, who has made him known" (John 1:18).

And this is why things got so interesting when Jesus came to earth. You see, God (the invisible God) had sent Jesus to fully reveal himself. Literally, God in the flesh. Paul reminds the Colossians that Jesus is "the image of the invisible God" (Colossians 1:15). Somehow God had actually pulled it off. He was actually able to enflesh himself in a human being.

And this wasn't a cut-rate semi-God. It's not like Jesus was some less-filling, "light" version of the Almighty. Paul assures us that *all of the fullness of God* dwelt in Jesus. And all of the fullness of God—all of it—was *pleased* to dwell in Jesus (Colossians 1:19). Apparently God was having a great time walking around with two feet and a head of hair.

And this was apparently an important point for Paul. Later in that same letter he reemphasizes that "in [Christ] the whole fullness of deity dwells bodily" (Colossians 2:9). And it's not just Paul who sees such significance in the incarnation. The author of Hebrews insists that the Son "is the reflection of God's glory and the exact imprint of God's very being" (Hebrews 1:3).

The apostle John tries to wrap words around this incarnation in another way. "In the beginning was the Word. . . . And the Word became flesh and lived among us" (John 1:1, 14). The Word (*logos* in Greek, meaning all logic, reason, reality—everything that has ever been true and real and resonated with the universe) took on meat (*sarx* in the Greek, literally flesh or skin). And that flesh is Jesus.

Jesus of Nazareth, the small-town carpenter, was the very flesh of the almighty, eternal, invisible God, Yahweh.

And as Jesus walked upon the earth, every decision he made, every lesson he taught, every conversation he had tells us about God. His posture, his manner of heart, his attitude, his outlook, his pace, his emotions, his death—all reveal God.

Every square inch of everything Jesus ever did speaks of God. His very life (not just his death) is utterly and simply sublime.

STARING AT THE FLESH

No wonder Paul—brilliant, urbane, educated Paul—wrote to the Corinthian church, "I decided to know nothing among you except Jesus Christ, and him crucified" (1 Corinthians 2:2). It wasn't that Paul felt that he had to dumb down his message for the Corinthians, leaving out essential lessons he didn't have time for. Paul felt that everything else was a distant second, almost irrelevant when compared to what was revealed in the person of Jesus. So he decided to know only Jesus among them.

That's quite a stand to take: for a scholar and leader like Paul to decide (to actively purpose) to know nothing other than Jesus and Jesus crucified. That kind of posture can make you look foolish. Or simple. Or silly. But Paul knew that next to knowing Jesus Christ and him crucified, all else paled in comparison.

So Paul became unabashedly centered on Jesus. He "fixed his eyes on Jesus," to use the language of Hebrews 12:2. Paul was a simpleton, when it comes right down to it. He wanted to know Jesus. And to know Jesus crucified. In the end nothing else mattered to him.

No wonder there's such a high JPS (Jesus per sentence) ratio in Paul's correspondence!

As an English major in college, I used to make fun of Paul's writing. His writing style seemed a bit repetitive, to say the least. He couldn't get a simple declarative sentence out of his mouth without mentioning Jesus at least a couple times.

For example, he starts his letter to the Philippians this way:

Paul and Timothy, servants of Christ Jesus,
To all the saints in Christ Jesus who are in Philippi, with the bishops and deacons:
Grace to you and peace from God our Father and the Lord Jesus Christ. (Philippians 1:1-2)

That's a three-to-one Jesus-per-sentence ratio, by my math. It's six to one if you count "Jesus" and "Christ" separately. Seems a bit over the top, doesn't it? And if you've read much Paul, you know this verse isn't an exception. Just in Philippians, Paul goes on to mention Jesus by name forty times. For a letter with only 104 verses, that's a lot of Jesus!

But maybe I was wrong in college. Maybe Paul wasn't a horrendous writer. Maybe he was just purposefully Jesus saturated. Maybe he was consumed with the person of Jesus.

After all, he did just love to go off about Jesus from time to time. Listen in as Paul tells the Colossians about Jesus:

He is the image of the invisible God, the firstborn of all creation; for in him all things in heaven and on earth were created, things visible and invisible, whether thrones or dominions or rulers or powers—all things have been created through him and for him. He himself is before all things, and in him all things hold together. He is the head of the body, the church; he is the beginning, the firstborn from the dead, so that he might come to have first place in everything. For in him all the fullness of God was pleased to dwell, and through him God was pleased to reconcile to himself all things, whether on earth or in heaven, by making peace through the blood of his cross. (Colossians 1:15-20)

Fun to read, isn't it? It's like Paul gets thinking about Jesus and just can't stop. This is the writing of a man who was fixated upon Jesus.

GUARDING THE TRUTH

And not only was Paul adamant about keeping himself centered on Jesus, he practically *insisted* that believers and churches everywhere be centered on Jesus as well.

Paul's primary leadership strategy was to get believers and Christian leaders everywhere to "guard the good treasure" (2 Timothy 1:14) about Jesus. He encouraged them to guard the truth not by hiding it away somewhere but by passing it on. His instructions were embarrassingly simple: tell other people what you've been told about Jesus.

Paul charged Timothy to teach about Jesus to faithful folks, who could teach about Jesus to other faithful folks, who . . . well, you get the picture (2 Timothy 2:1-2). Paul urges Titus to pick leaders for his church who could hold strongly to what they had been taught, not straying at all from what they were told (Titus 1:9). Good memory, in other words—the ability to hold steadfastly to the clear image of Jesus that had been presented to them, so that they could pass that image on.

And that's church. Transmitting from person to person the truth about Jesus. For Paul, remaining centered on Jesus was of the utmost importance. Maintaining a clear view of Jesus was the role of the church.

And it wasn't just Paul who felt strongly about this. It's impossible to read the New Testament as a whole and not pick up on the strong emphasis on holding tightly to the truth about Jesus exactly as it had been received. The author of Hebrews is adamant: "We must pay greater attention to what we have heard, so that we do not drift away from it" (Hebrews 2:1). John states it clearly: "Let what you heard from the beginning abide in you" (1 John 2:24).

If a clear picture of Jesus was so central to the early church, then no wonder the Gospels were written. No wonder false gospels were so quickly identified and spoken out against. No wonder the church was led by God to canonize the Gospels that truly recorded the life and steps and ways of Jesus as well as the story of his crucifixion and resurrection.

No wonder Paul wrote to Timothy and told him to "remember Jesus" (2 Timothy 2:8).

Remember Jesus? That's right—Paul wrote to Timothy and actually told him to "remember Jesus." Let's keep the context of this letter straight here: Paul is writing to Timothy, the leader of the Christian church of an entire city, a future bishop no less. And he tells him to *remember Jesus*. What an interesting charge to put in his letter to Timothy! I believe this one comment by Paul is either the greatest understatement I've ever read or some of the greatest, most sublime theology I've ever encountered.

And I personally don't think it was an understatement. I think Paul understood that the primary task of every church leader was to keep the church centered upon Jesus Christ. I think he was being wise and shrewd and loving by calling Timothy to have his eyes fixed upon Jesus.

No wonder John took such great joy in passing on to others what he had seen in Jesus. He was the last apostle alive who had seen Jesus with his own eyes. Listen to how he begins his first letter: "We declare to you what was from the beginning, what we have heard, what we have seen with our eyes, what we have looked at and touched with our hands, concerning the word of life—this life was revealed, and we have seen it and testify to it" (1 John 1:1-2). John's life was forever altered by seeing God in the flesh, and he couldn't help but want to tell others exactly what he saw and heard and even touched.

He ends his opening paragraph with a fun confession: "We are writing these things so that our joy may be complete" (1 John 1:4). What a great mercy from God that the mere act of passing on this image of Jesus to future generations is enjoyable!

But of course it is, for we are speaking about a clear picture of the very flesh of our invisible God.

No wonder the earliest Christian hymns were all about Jesus. No wonder the church sang of his life (he "emptied himself, taking the form of a slave") and his death ("he humbled himself and became obedient to the point of death—even death on a cross," Philippians 2:7-8).

The early church tells us that the role of the church in every age is to guard the truth about Jesus' life and death by receiving the image of Jesus that's been guarded before us and then passing it on, unaltered, to the next generation through songs and sermons and conversations and letters.

BEING CENTERED ON JESUS TODAY

Seeing Paul's and John's and the rest of the gang's preoccupation with Jesus should make us sit up and take notice. Their focus on Jesus is relentless and unquestionable and on purpose. Their insistence that the church be centered upon Jesus is clear and strong and repeated.

And their strong insistence that the church focus on Jesus isn't a heavy burden. It's a welcome invitation. It's very good news. If we get to see the fullness of God in the life of Jesus, why *not* nuzzle up for a close look? Why not become preoccupied with the stories of his life? Why not fix our collective eyes upon him? If this man is the image of the invisible God—the actual flesh of the God whom humans have sought to comprehend and know since the dawn of time—then who could blame us for becoming preoccupied with this God-man?

Let there be no mistake: the call to focus on Jesus is a call to life. I've been a campus minister since 1994 and have been teaching campus fellowships, counseling students, meeting with non-Christian students, debating atheists, praying with freshmen and leading other staff for all of my adult life. Though I realize I am young and my experience is limited, I have learned two hard truths during my time on campus: (1) The world—including me—is beautiful and broken and confused. (2) In Jesus we have the answer to almost every question or dilemma or opportunity we will ever face on this earth.

I have found that the more I focus upon Jesus, the more fruit and clarity I see in my own life and in my ministry among students. The more clever and sophisticated and unfocused I become, the less life there is in me and in those I minister among and the more muddled our ministry becomes. And I don't think that's a coincidence. As I read the New Testament, I see in Paul and Peter and the rest of the gang a real insight and brilliance that insists that the church be fixated upon Jesus.

I think their focus on Jesus was a move of pure genius. And I think their posture should make us ask some serious questions about where our own eyes are fixed and how much we pay attention to the life of Jesus.

For example, are we teaching about both the life *and* death of Jesus in our churches? Remember that Paul purposed to know Jesus Christ (his person and life and teachings) *and* him crucified (his work on the cross). Are we careful to do the same in our worship services? Or are we reducing our teaching about Jesus to his work on the cross only? Of course his death and resurrection are central and beautiful and sublime. But so is the *life* of Jesus.

It's significant that the Gospels themselves don't merely tell the story of Jesus' death. They tell the story (in great detail, in fact) of Jesus' life. How he lived, where he went, who he talked to, how he treated people, what he taught. The invisible God was actually walking around with skin on, after all! The Gospels don't just tell the story of Jesus crucified. And neither should we.

Are the songs of our congregations fully Jesus centered? In worship, do we celebrate the life of Jesus: his humility while on earth, his deep compassion for the poor, his searing parables? Or do we only celebrate his death and work on the cross, cutting ourselves off from the full revelation from God that we have in Jesus?

Are our sermons and Bible studies and talks focused on the life and death of Jesus? If someone came to our church only one week, are we confident that he or she would hear about Jesus? Or are we getting caught up in themes or issues or controversies that pull us away from the central point of our existence as communities: the life and death of Jesus?

Are our leaders preoccupied and enamored with Jesus, as Paul was? Are we choosing leaders because of their affection for Jesus, because we are confident that they will keep us centered upon him? Or do we get caught up in the education and giftedness and charisma and overall pedigree of our leaders?

Are we, like the early church, preoccupied with Jesus? Or have we become too sophisticated? Too comprehensive? Too relevant? Too clever?

I remember clearly the first time I sat through a church service without hearing about Jesus. He wasn't even mentioned. I was a young believer at the time and was shocked. Appalled. Confused.

But as time has gone on, I've sat through many church services and realized that my initial experience wasn't as much of an anomaly as I had hoped. And I realized that within me, too, was this tendency to stray, to fade in focus, to have wandering eyes.

As I wrestle with my own tendency to have bad eyes, eyes that can't focus on Jesus, I have come upon a question that helps me understand where my eyes are and how clever I have grown. It's a potentially dangerous question I think anyone can ask.

You should know, by the way, that I like questions that bother and pester. Questions that hang around and haunt me even after I give them an appropriate answer. I consider these to be "potentially dangerous" questions because they just might make room for God to speak into our lives. So in each chapter I want to ask at least one potentially dangerous question.

POTENTIALLY DANGEROUS QUESTION 1: *If I received a letter or e-mail from a friend encouraging me to "remember Jesus," how would that make me feel?*

Would I feel thankful? Convicted? Encouraged? Indignant? Insulted? Misunderstood? Would I think that my friend was being a little too simplistic? Too naive? Too cartoonish in his or her theology? Or would I receive it gratefully? Thankful to have my cleverness challenged and my eyes brought back to Jesus, the center of life itself?

It's a telling question to ponder, because how that call to "remember Jesus" sounds to my ears tells me a lot about the state of my soul and of my eyes.

———————

Oh, to be a generation that is faithful to our task of guarding the truth. To be a church that is unabashedly centered on Jesus. To be unembarrassed about our preoccupation with him. To have his name come easily and often to our lips.

To have our eyes focused solidly upon him. Really fixed upon him. To have leaders who call our attention back to Jesus again and again and again. To be able to call our leaders to remember Jesus without worrying about being seen as overly simplistic.

Oh, for a church that dives headlong into this great, sublime, New Testament theology that proclaims Jesus, and him crucified, above all else.

Oh, to be simpletons. Yes, simpletons. Simpletons who, like Paul, have purposed to know nothing but Jesus. Simpletons whose message, like Paul's, is utterly Jesus saturated. Simpletons who tap into the greatest revelation of all time—God in the flesh.

May we relearn how to stare at you, Jesus.

Chapter Two
Blurry Jesus

Despite our calling as a church, it is difficult to maintain a clear view of Jesus.

Mighty difficult. Always has been, always will be. Ever since Jesus first walked the earth, there has been a sure, steady attack upon the truth about his life and death.

This shouldn't be too surprising, of course. If Jesus is the image of the invisible God, then God's enemy is going to be very interested in blurring that image. Clarity is the last thing our enemy is interested in. He hates clarity. Abhors it. In teaching about Satan (a name that literally means "adversary") Jesus called him "the father of lies" (John 8:44).

The Liar, I like to call him. Sure, calling him Satan clarifies that we have an enemy, but calling him The Liar clarifies what his primary weapon is: deception. Deception is his game. And if the incarnation of God in Jesus was God's greatest, most concentrated effort in history at revealing himself, then it would stand to reason that God's adversary, The Liar, would attack that image with his greatest, most concentrated efforts at deception.

And so it has been. According to Paul, "the god of this world has blinded the minds of unbelievers, to keep them from seeing the light of the gospel of the glory of Christ, who is the image of God" (2 Corinthians 4:4). The Liar busies himself with blinding people to the image of God. And so in every age the church's picture of Jesus has come under attack.

Some attacks have been frontal assaults. Others have been subtle, mere whispers to catch the church off guard. But all of them are dangerous, for they threaten the perfect image of God that we have in the person of Jesus and in every step he took.

It would be impossible for me to address all of these attacks. They are so numerous and varied, so strong and convincing, so subtle and almost invisible at times. Thankfully, this is the task of the church—to discern deception wherever it appears and to confront it with the truth about Jesus.

As for me, in over a decade of ministry on college campuses in the United States, I have encountered many deceptions about Jesus—both in the students and in myself. But three areas of deception have stood out to me as particularly dangerous: outright lies, home blindness and religious language. Let's consider each of these areas of deception as illustrations of just how easy it is for the truth about Jesus to become blurred.

HOLOGRAM JESUS AND OTHER LIES

There's nothing new about outright lies. There have always been folks who spread lies about Jesus.

Whether well meaning or not, whether directly motivated by The Liar or not, some folks get the story wrong and yet spread it nonetheless.

For example, the Gnostics were philosophical intellectuals who held great sway in the first centuries after Jesus' ascension. Because their philosophy embraced a dualistic view of the universe (there's physical stuff, which is bad, and spiritual stuff, which is good), they couldn't accept that Jesus was God and in a human body. The idea of the God-man created a tension in their worldview that just made them shiver!

So they relieved that tension by dropping the man part. They proposed that Jesus was actually a hologram, an apparition. He was a sort of God projection that looked like a body but wasn't really human. This teaching about Jesus actually started to catch on.

Now, it just wasn't true. Jesus was human. His body was real. And there are many texts in the New Testament that guarantee as much. Nonetheless, this Gnostic teaching caught on. And folks' image of Jesus eroded a bit. And The Liar grinned and chuckled.

And thus it is. In every age there are going to be influential people who, for whatever reason, put forth wrong ideas about Jesus.

In our own day this remains true. For example, the idea of the God-man remains offensive. Some folks these days try to ease that tension by dropping the God part. Jesus was just a man, a teacher. The miracle stories, therefore, are quite unlikely and must have been fabricated. This progressive belief about Jesus has caught on as a handy way to relieve the tension inherent in the God-man concept. So books are written, scholarly symposiums are held and (eventually but sadly) sermons are preached proclaiming such a distorted message about Jesus.

This man-only view is no more true than the Gnostics' God-only belief. The witness of Scripture does not allow the miraculous to be stripped away from Jesus. There is a fabric of testimony about Jesus in the Gospels that is of one piece. No one story or aspect of Jesus can be cut out of the fabric, for nothing coherent would be left. It all holds or falls together.

Even so, this false idea about Jesus' divine nature has caught on and our collective image of Jesus has taken a blow. The truth about Jesus has become that much more out of focus. It would probably make Paul faint. John would likely reason with us that he had seen Jesus and heard him and *touched* him. That he had seen the miracles with his very own eyes! Why would we reject his testimony for the story of those who weren't even there?

But so it is. Each age is faced with deceptions, lies and confusions about Jesus' ways and teachings and person. The outright lies may vary greatly in content and delivery and style. But the effect is always the same—the truth is distorted rather than guarded.

HOW A BIG, UGLY PILLOW CAN DISAPPEAR

Other than bald-faced lies, these days we also have something that has been called "home blindness" to worry about. Over the years, home blindness has taken a subtle but undeniable swipe at our image of Jesus.

Being home blind is a phenomenon we've all experienced. It's when we are so used to something being around that we stop seeing it in detail. Psychologists affirm that this is a universal experience and a natural, functional response of the human brain.

Whether we're talking about a picture hanging on the wall, the patterns of tile in the bathroom or the color of a chair, we all have items we've become "home blind" to. We see something so often that our brains stop taking note of the details.

And you can't know it's happening until you see the object in a new light, out of context or from someone else's perspective. Then the details come flooding back in. This is how our brains work.

I have a huge pillow that my mom made for me when I was a kid. It was larger than me when I first got it, and I dubbed it *The TV Pillow*. I would ride it like a horse, sit on it while watching TV, throw it at my brother. It was always around. For years. So much so that I stopped really seeing it. Whenever it was in my field of vision, I didn't take in the various details of the pillow; my mind just registered, *TV Pillow.*

It wasn't until I got married that I actually saw my pillow in detail again. My new wife (with a concerned but polite look on her face) asked me what we were "going to do about that TV pillow." When I asked her what she meant, she explained how the ugly, painfully out-of-date brown and gray paisley patterns and the multiple busted seams made it suspect from an interior decorating point of view.

I was shocked at her words. *My TV pillow isn't ugly and brown!* I rushed off to get the pillow to prove her wrong. But sure enough, it *was* brown and gray. And it *was* coming apart at the seams. And it was ugly. I was incredulous. When did my TV pillow become ugly?

So it is as humans. Over time, familiarity can breed blindness.

And nowhere is this more disastrous than when it comes to Jesus. We can be so smothered with religious phrases about Jesus, so accustomed to the stories of his life that we start losing the details. When a Gospel story starts being read to us, our active minds sort of switch off and all of the details are lost on us. A vague, iconic image of Jesus is all we can see.

I've not only experienced this myself, I have seen it in those around me time and time again.

One fall evening a few years ago I sat on a dingy green carpet in a dorm room on the University of Colorado campus. Sitting with me were a half dozen freshmen eager to begin our first Bible study of the school year. To my right was a young woman who had come from a Christian home and was excited to have found a group of Christians at her new school. After announcing the chapter and verse numbers for our study and asking everyone to read it through a couple times on their own, I saw the young woman flip to the right verses, scan the page and then close her Bible with a nod.

For the next two hours we sat around talking about Jesus' interactions with the lawyer and the ensuing parable about the good Samaritan. Many in the group had never read the story before. And yet it was the young woman to my right who time and time again got the story wrong, mixed up the characters and caused the new believers in the room to look puzzled and glance back at their texts to clarify what was happening in the story.

They were confused by her inattention to detail. I was not. I knew that she had begun to *assume* the story, to allow it to slip into that part of her mind that rubs out all details and leaves only a vague, cartoonish story in its place. It wasn't something she'd done on purpose, of course. She had just heard the good Samaritan story so many times that she had become home blind to it. The details were lost on her. Actually, the whole story and all it revealed about Jesus (and therefore God) had become lost to her as well. It took the new believers around her, seeing the story for the first time, for her to really see the story again.

There is nothing remarkable about her story. I've seen it lived out in dozens of other dorm rooms with hundreds of other students.

And while this story may seem funny, this dulling of our senses is not a laughing matter. It blurs our view of Jesus and steadily erodes the truth that we're supposed to be guarding. Though the pages of the Gospels are bursting with glorious details about Jesus, though there's more there than we could ever fully see and comprehend and master, our minds click into home blindness at some point and our collective view of Jesus suffers for it. Instead of guarding the truth, we allow it to blur into vagueness.

And The Liar chuckles and wrings his hands with glee. Our eyes glaze over and his eyes grow wide with pleasure. We yawn and he smiles.

A MASS OF LATIN WORDS

When it comes to maintaining a clear view of Jesus, the nature of modern language in America doesn't help us out much, either.

George Orwell noticed a significant turn in our country's use of language more than fifty years ago. He explained, "There is a trend in modern language away from concreteness."[1] He illustrated this trend by translating Ecclesiastes 9:11 into "modern" English. First, here is the traditional, King James version of that verse:

> I returned, and saw under the sun, that the race is not to the swift, nor the battle to the strong, neither yet bread to the wise, nor yet riches to men of understanding, nor yet favour to men of skill; but time and chance happeneth to them all.

Compare that with Orwell's version:

> Objective consideration of contemporary phenomena compels the conclusion that success or failure in competitive activities exhibits no tendency to be commensurate with innate capacity, but that a considerable element of the unpredictable must invariably be taken into account.[2]

Now this "modern translation" is pretty humorous to read, but Orwell was not trying to be funny. He goes on to do a careful analysis of the older English version and the modern English version and eventually comes to what seems to me a chilling conclusion: "The first sentence contains six vivid images . . . the second contains not a single fresh, arresting phrase, and in spite of its ninety syllables it gives only a shortened version of the meaning contained in the first."[3]

As it turns out, modern language may sound more sophisticated, may strike someone as more impressive, but the reality is that it contains *less actual meaning* than language that is anchored in the basic, real stuff of life. Sophistication in language often dulls meaning. And we live in a day when sophisticated language reigns. This is a sad state for the cause of clarity.

As Orwell put it so finely, "A mass of Latin words falls upon the facts like soft snow, blurring the outlines and covering up all the details."[4]

This shift in language may seem subtle and unimportant, but I submit that the effects of this trend in language have sadly added to the Jesus blur we suffer from. We live in an age when clarity, detail and precision are sacrificed (perhaps unknowingly) to sophistication, pride and vagueness. And I'm sure The Liar has no problem with this trend. He may not have caused it, but deception in any form is water to his parched throat.

I think he would be especially pleased that the halls of Christian theology have adopted this trend in modern language silently and completely. And the result is that our vernacular as a church has become sophisticated and therefore dulled in real meaning. We have been handed a palette of words that we use to describe our faith, our devotions, our church life and our Savior, Jesus. The only problem is that this set of religious words, in their modern sophistication, can actually obscure our message.

To borrow from Orwell, I contend that our lofty theological words and time-honored stereotypes and clichés have fallen upon Jesus like soft snow, blurring his outlines and covering up the details.

And what a damnable turn for matters to take, for our clear picture of Jesus gets rubbed and blurred with a string of long, thick theological words. We tell the world of a "divine Savior who brought ultimate and eternal salvation for fallen humanity" and the world just blinks. We sing of our "blessed Redeemer whose substitutionary death imputes righteousness" and have to stifle our *own* yawns. And the words float away on lofty wings, too high for us to really hear and grasp them.

And we are left with a vague picture of Jesus, unable to fully guard the truth that's been handed down throughout the centuries.

GUARDING THE TRUTH TODAY

Lies, blinding familiarity and a trend in language that frustrates clarity. Indeed it is mighty difficult to hear, let alone guard, the truth about Jesus. And it's not like these are the only image-distorting deceptions we battle with these days.

Everything from sloppy language to cultural biases to wounds caused by Christians can also blur our image of Jesus. As Søren Kierkegaard lamented, "The modern age has abolished Christ. . . . Essentially Christ is remodeled."[5] And that makes it difficult for the church to do what the church is supposed to do: guard the truth about the miraculous revelation we have in the life of Jesus.

What's a church to do?

Well, the good news is we're not alone in this struggle to maintain clarity about Jesus. Paul and John and Timothy and the rest of the gang faced similar struggles. I think this is why they were centered upon and preoccupied with Jesus. I think this is why folks from Paul on down have always had to be vigilant and purposeful about keeping the truth about Jesus from being blurred. They've had to be diligent to guard the truth that had been handed to them.

They were like simpletons who knew only one thing—Jesus. And it was in their simplicity that they were able to confound the strategies of The Liar, who sought at every turn to distort their true picture of Jesus.

The early church's purposeful, desperate preoccupation with and focus upon Jesus proved to be a brilliant move. A true grace of God. Their focus on guarding the truth was their lifeblood.

Which makes me think of another haunting question to introduce into our lives.

POTENTIALLY DANGEROUS QUESTION 2: *Why is it that each season of ingathering that the church has seen has been marked by a renewed centrality and focus upon Jesus?*

Consider a recent example: the Jesus Movement in America during the 1960s and 1970s. It was a great season of renewal for the church, a great ingathering of people, a time of real life in God's church. And it was a time marked by a focus on Jesus. Hippies weren't streaming into the kingdom because of clever clergy and snazzy church buildings. They were hearing about Jesus. And they liked what they saw in him.

Thus is the story of the church in every season marked by new life and vibrancy and renewal. As Dr. Martyn Lloyd-Jones observed, "If you turn to the historical evidence and read the accounts of all the revivals that have ever been known in the long history of the church, you will find invariably that the very centre of the life of the church, at that time, has been the Lord Jesus Christ himself."[6] Thus was the story of the early church as described in Acts.

And today's church? Well, what else can we do but try to be simpletons? To be centered on Jesus. To try to hear the story right and say it right. To guard the truth that's been handed to us. To speak of Jesus often, to become Jesus consumed like Paul and John.

This little book is an attempt to re-encounter and tell the truth about Jesus. The study pursued in these pages is simple and specifically aimed at the struggles we face today. As a member of the church, I offer up my humble attempt at hearing the story right and saying it right.

But how to hear the story right despite all that's working against us? First, I knew that to see Jesus clearly I would need to be rooted in Scripture. In a world of lies, where else do you turn for a starting place?

But that's not good enough in itself, because home blindness renders so much of that Scripture dull and unintelligible to my ears and eyes. So I needed to find Scripture about Jesus that I wasn't very familiar with. Anything that had ever been put on a bathroom plaque or honored in stained glass would be of no use for this study.

Finally, I knew I had to stay away from long words. The rut of modern language is just so deep and close at hand that I knew that any language that sounded theological or sophisticated in the least bit wouldn't be helpful to me. I needed small words. About simple, earthy things.

So the task was simple: find Scripture about Jesus that I wasn't very familiar with and that was not overtly religious or theological sounding. And do you know what? I found some. But what I found has not only allowed me to see Jesus more clearly than ever, it has changed my life. For a stubborn young guy who loves comfort and abhors transformation, that says a lot.

BLUE-COLLAR SCRIPTURE

I began my search in the "black verses" of the Gospels.

You know the ones I'm talking about—the ones that aren't in red. Yeah, those. It was a simple strategy, even a bit silly, I guess. I figured they were in the Gospels so they counted as being in Scripture and must have something to do with Jesus, thus meeting my first test.

I also figured that the red verses of the Gospels (the words and teachings of Jesus) had received most of our attention, leaving these black verses more ignored and less eroded by home blindness. After all, how many black verses have been painstakingly illuminated by monks or carefully memorized by kids going through confirmation classes? This satisfied my second test.

Finally, I combed through the black verses, taking out anything that sounded blatantly theological. If it sounded lofty enough to be at home in a hymn or worship song, I dispensed with it for the purposes of this study.

In the end what I found were some really boring verses.

Seemingly boring, anyway. Common verses. With plain words. They are what I consider the "stage directions" of the Gospels. Verses that tell what happened in between all the action. Verses like these: "And they were all amazed at what Jesus had said." "Then Jesus took the blind man by the hand and led him out of town." "He fell at Jesus' feet." "They brought all the sick to Jesus."

No quotes, just descriptions of what's happening around the main action. Helpful if you're making a screenplay but not the usual fodder for worship songs or sermons or memorization. Blue-collar verses, I guess. Simple words that describe earthy things.

Yet these blue-collar verses are there in the pages of the Gospels. And they didn't have to be. They may seem like unimportant verses, but they were recorded. And there are a lot of them. It's significant, I began to realize, that in the Gospels we don't just have a bullet list of quotes from Jesus. We have stories of the way Jesus was, how folks responded to him, who touched whom, where folks went and how folks dealt with Jesus.

SURPRISED BY SIMPLE VERSES

The more time I spent in these blue-collar verses, the more I realized they weren't really boring at all. In fact, themes started to emerge. Powerful themes that surprised me. Almost shocked me. Caught me off-guard. I had read these verses before, of course, during various Bible studies, but they had never really struck my eyes as significant.

But when I got enough of these boring verses together, Jesus seemed to jump right off the page in ways he never had before. I saw new sides of him—his strangeness, his mercy, his brilliance, his sacrificial nature. And there's just something about seeing Jesus clearly. It makes your heart pound and your eyes grow wide and you find yourself living differently.

As I was caught up in the person of Jesus, I began to understand more and more why Paul had made that decision of his to focus on Jesus alone. To know nothing but Jesus is to choose to stare at an image that ignites something deep within you. His life and ways and manner called forth a response from within me that I couldn't have mustered on my own. It's like the flesh of God began to come into focus. And that clarity changed me.

The remaining chapters lay out some of these blue-collar verses for you to roam through. Perhaps they'll catch you off guard as well.

————————

Oh, may we all see Jesus more clearly every year. May our two-dimensional, cartoonish pictures of Jesus get more and more real flesh put on them as we consider the Gospel records of Jesus. May our Father help us fight off the lies and deceptions that The Liar pelts us with so regularly.

May the life of Jesus that has been so blurred over time, so muddied by this world, so splattered with false words and subtle deceptions, come crisply into focus.

May our return to the plain words of the Gospels help us clear our heads and see with more clarity. May today's church hear the story right. And may we, like the apostle John, take great joy in passing that story on.

Book Two
The Presence of Jesus

As Jesus walked the dusty streets of Israel, many people were overcome by his presence among them. Some were shocked and stunned. Others worshiped him on the spot.

What was it in his presence that made them react in these ways? And what difference does that make for us today?

Chapter Three
They Were Seized by Amazement

One of the first themes that jumped out at me when I began to study the stage directions of the Gospels was how many gaping jaws there were. Left and right we see folks standing around Jesus, amazed. Women shocked. Old men staring. Enemies intrigued.

Listen to this stunning chorus found within the stage directions of the Gospels.

They were amazed, saying, "What sort of man is this?" (Matthew 8:27)

The crowds were amazed and said, "Never has anything like this been seen in Israel." (Matthew 9:33)

All the crowds were amazed. (Matthew 12:23)

They were greatly astounded. (Matthew 19:25)

They were all amazed and glorified God, saying, "We have never seen anything like this!" (Mark 2:12)

They were overcome with amazement. (Mark 5:42)

They were utterly astounded. (Mark 6:51)

They were greatly astounded. (Mark 10:26)

They were amazed, and those who followed were afraid. (Mark 10:32)

Pilate was amazed. (Mark 15:5)

Everyone was amazed at all that he was doing. (Luke 9:43)

Amazement seized all of them, and they glorified God and were filled with awe, saying, "We have seen strange things today." (Luke 5:26)

And that's just a short sampling. Everywhere Jesus went, folks were surprised. And this is noteworthy. It's a theme worth paying attention to.

Given how cynical and dulled of senses we can be as a species, it's significant that Jesus caused shock everywhere he went. If we saw only a few shocked people in the Gospels, it would be nothing worthy of note. But what do you do with whole crowds that are shocked? What about multitudes standing with gaping jaws?

And don't you think it's remarkable that those who recorded these Gospels felt it was necessary to record this part of the story? This chorus of amazement must be significant. But what does it teach us about Jesus?

THE MOOSE IN HIM

Let's focus in on that last verse, Luke 5:26. Pulling back to look at the context, we see that it's been a pretty typical day for Jesus. He teaches all day in a house crowded with his disciples, the curious and a gaggle of sworn enemies who are looking for dirt on him. During that day, Jesus heals a man, forgives sin, responds to outspoken critics of the healing and forgiveness. A Jesus kind of day. The kind of day we're used to reading about. But at the end of that day, we're told, "Amazement seized all of them, and they glorified God and were filled with awe, saying, 'We have seen strange things today'" (Luke 5:26).

I've begun to really like this little verse from Luke 5. It's such an intriguing, full sentence that can potentially tell us so much about Jesus. As when reading a good poem, the more we stop to listen to this verse, to ask questions of it, the more loudly it speaks.

What does it mean, for example, that amazement seized everyone there? I can imagine being amazed or intrigued or interested, but being "seized" by amazement? That sounds kind of extreme. In the Greek, too, the "all of them" is the *object* of the sentence, not the *subject*. The people weren't in control. They were being caught up by something else. How did spending a day with Jesus make everyone get caught up by amazement like that?

And how about that "all of them"? In Greek there are two words you could use to say "all": *pantas* and *hapantas*. They're the same word, except one has a syllable of great emphasis (*ha*) added on. You use that one, *hapantas*, when you're wanting to emphasize that it really was everyone. And this is the one Luke uses here. Luke is emphasizing that "all of them" were seized by amazement—even the enemies who came there to purposefully look for dirt on Jesus.

That would be like a Republican journalist going to a Democratic convention for some juicy sound bites and leaving utterly caught up in what was going on there. That would never happen, right? But it did with Jesus' enemies after spending a day with him. How can that be? What was it in Jesus that so caught them off guard that their stiff, defensive posture melted away into amazement?

Luke also tells us that they glorified God and were filled with fear at the same time. At the same time! What was it in Jesus that made them worship God *and* be really afraid? And what was it that made them sit around afterward chatting away about the "strange things" they'd seen that day?

If this little verse tells us anything, it tells us that being in the same room with Jesus was an intense experience.

I've grown to really like this verse and what it clarifies about Jesus. And never did it hold such meaning for me than after an intimate encounter I had with a moose recently in the Rocky Mountains of Colorado.

I was at a condo near Breckenridge with a dozen good friends. We were sitting in the living room studying Acts. Minding our own business. Having a wonderful, polite conversation as we sat in the morning sun coming in from the large sliding-glass door.

But just like that, we all looked up from our Bibles at the same time. We stared at each other for a second, and I felt a sort of presence in the room and could tell that everyone else was feeling the same thing. Then, without anyone's saying a word, we all slowly turned our heads toward the sliding-glass door (I am not making any of this up!) and there, staring back at us, was the largest moose I had ever seen.

A side note about moose is in order here. Moose are large. Really large. Pictures never do them justice. In pictures they just look like large horses with strange, flattened antlers. But when you see a moose up close (especially if it is on the other side of your sliding-glass door), you realize how mammoth these animals are. Our moose, for example, was so immense that its legs were standing on the ground *below* our large deck but it was still tall enough and long enough to get its large face and antlers right up to our sliding-glass door. Without even using the bottom step for a boost!

Enough about moose. Suffice it to say that having one stare at you from the other side of a frighteningly thin sliding-glass door is enough to take over a room. No one asked for permission to halt our study in Acts (I remember, I was leading), no one asked what we should do, no one used the break to go to the bathroom. We all just jumped up and were drawn to the moose. It was so large, its nostrils so huge, its flattened antler things so wide and looming that we were strangely drawn to it. "Look at its nostrils!" we whispered in awe while slowly tiptoeing toward it.

Then it snorted. And we all jumped back. A few screamed. I peed my pants. A little. For the minute that we stared at this intense animal and it stared back, I never blinked. The feeling in the room was electric.

Then all of a sudden, obviously bored with our wide eyes and gaping jaws, it turned slowly and romped (there is no other verb to use here) through the trees and was seen no more.

We staggered back into the living room. And with silly grins and uncontrollable energy, we spent the next thirty minutes jabbering like schoolgirls about how amazing it was. "Did you see how it knocked over those small trees as it just . . . romped away?" "Dude, did you see how tall its legs were? I could have walked right under its belly!" "No way that just happened!"

And I have never read Luke 5:26 the same way again.

Luke's description of the crowd in this verse clarifies for me how being around Jesus was like being around this moose. There was something in Jesus—in his mere manner and presence—that caught people off guard and swept them up in his very being.

When you encounter something with an intense presence (be it Messiah or moose), you are no longer in control. You are taken, seized by the magnificence and sheer size of what you are witnessing. We did not choose, on that Colorado morning, to stop our study and go over to the screen door. We were "seized by amazement," taken up in the presence of the moose. How striking that simple Jesus, as he went about his ministry, had this same effect on people. Even on his enemies.

And there's something about a large, surprising presence that is both impressive and scary. On that bright morning we had praise just issuing from us ("It's so amazing!" "Did you see its ear twitch?") and yet we were definitely (trust me on this one) full of fear. Luke tells us that this is exactly the effect that Jesus had on everyone in the crowd that day. They worshiped and were afraid. This tells us something about Jesus' presence, doesn't it?

And then, at the end of the day with Jesus, everyone there (remember, enemies and all) sat around chatting about all they had seen. An experience with a new, shocking presence can do that to you. I remember that it was with great effort that I eventually refocused our eyes on Acts that morning in Colorado. We just kept talking about that moose with silly grins on our faces.

Luke describes a shocked, amazed crowd. Jesus, like a moose, had wandered into their presence that day and had left them staring with gaping jaws, wondering just what had happened. And this instance in Luke 5 isn't even exceptional. Each Gospel writer records the shock and amazement of the crowds around Jesus multiple times. It seems this was the norm when Jesus walked into a town.

Jesus was strange and different and shocking. And people couldn't help but stare. That is the story that the Gospels tell again and again. It is safe to say that, of all the things Jesus saw on human faces as he walked this earth, dropped jaws was one of them. It was as if one sustained gasp followed Jesus wherever he went. Never did what you thought he was going to do. Never said what you assumed he would say. Never sought out those you would have guessed. Never avoided those you assumed he would. He was a strange man, this carpenter.

In a word, Jesus was utterly holy. Yeah, *holy*.

The word *holy* means "set apart, separate from the everyday, other." And in the Gospel pages we see that holiness dripped from Jesus' every move and daily decision. He was different. He was *not like us*. That's the sense of the word *holy*.

Jesus was not like anything on earth. And that makes a difference. That is theologically significant. Seeing Jesus' holiness brings our picture of Jesus into greater focus. And seeing Jesus clearly, I believe, makes all the difference in the world.

STARE AT HIM

What do you do with the holy? With the strange and shocking and new?

Why, you can't help but be riveted on it! It attracts your attention, and without shame or embarrassment, you stare. You just stare. You can't help it when you're around such a presence. You are just drawn to it.

Jesus told his disciples that prophets and kings had longed to see what they were getting to see: God come upon the earth, walking around in utter holiness (Luke 10:24). If rulers and men of great power and control leaned across the pages of history, longing for a glimpse of Jesus walking upon the earth, then we shouldn't feel embarrassed if he so captures our attention too.

We should go ahead and stare. Gaze upon his life and be enthralled.

We should grab a copy of a Gospel, sit under a tree and read. Spend an afternoon breathing in the foreign air of Jesus. We should let ourselves roam through Jesus' little parables and let them shock us. We should allow ourselves to so study the life of Jesus that we become captivated and entrenched in the subtle details and intense themes we find there.

We should hold church services that relentlessly pull our eyes back to him, the center of our faith. We should lift up his name

often and speak to each other about how his life and manner have
been affecting us lately.

We should keep a growing list by our bedside of how Jesus impressed us during the day or of what we especially like about him.
We should be so convinced of his holiness, his strangeness, that
we never make the mistake of assuming things about him or
growing bored with the stories of his life.

We should always be working through a Gospel from front to
back, allowing ourselves to walk through every part of his life, to
consider every teaching of his, rather than always focusing on
what we already like or remember about him.

We should, like Paul, become simpletons who find at the center of our every thought and action the person of Jesus. We
should become indignant if we ever sit through a church service
without hearing of Jesus. We should become so used to staring at
Jesus that if he is removed from our view for too long, we notice.
And are bothered.

What do you do with the holy? You stare at it.

Sounds simple enough. But it's not always that easy, is it? It's
actually quite challenging to remain focused on Jesus. And why
is it so hard?

It's hard to remain focused on Jesus because we become too
sophisticated. The Gospels are so simple and straightforward
that we sort of *graduate* on to Paul. Where the meaty theology lies.
We hand the Gospels over to our children for their Sunday school
classes and move on to headier themes in our adult education.

We move on. Silently, subtly. Barely noticeable at first. But this
move can eventually take us down a road to a place where we find
it awkward to talk about Jesus in real, relational language. *What
do you like about Jesus these days?* can become an awkward question
to respond to. It sort of hangs in the air: silly, simple and nearly
unintelligible to our sophisticated faith.

It's difficult to remain focused on Jesus because we too often give in to a culture that gags on Jesus. Over time we let his name slip from our vernacular. Jesus has always been a stumbling block. Even his name grates on worldly human ears. Remember the assembly gathered against Peter and John in Acts 4? Their one request: just stop speaking to people in this name! There's something about Jesus, even his name, that is anathema to this world.

Even today our neighbors seem allergic to his name. They will nod and smile and listen to us talk of religion and God and faith and spirituality and even Christ from time to time. But mention Jesus and the conversation is over. And so we relent over time. Using other words. Focusing on other gospel themes. Until we find ourselves in such a place that Jesus is foreign to our language of faith, foreign to our worship services.

It's also difficult to remain focused on Jesus because there are so many other interesting, compelling things to focus on instead. Maybe we don't *replace* Jesus as our focus (that would be too explicitly unevangelical of us), but we just may allow others topics to "share" our focus. Which, to get technical, isn't really focusing at all, is it?

So we become all about Jesus and the end times. And our curriculum shifts, ever so slightly, away from the person of Jesus. Or maybe it's Jesus and gifts of the Spirit, or Jesus and church growth theory, or Jesus and worship styles. It doesn't matter what specifically we are tempted to focus on, it's the trying to focus on two things at once that enters us into dangerous ground.

Of course we will, rightly, take certain points and theologies and issues into our hands from time to time. It can be good to think about gifts. It can be good to think about church growth. But to have our eyes become at all preoccupied with those things is dangerous. We could end up with unhealthy eyes.

Jesus taught that the main reason people in his own day

didn't recognize him was because they had "unhealthy eyes" (Luke 11:29-36). His suggestion: have healthy eyes (or *single* eyes, as it's sometimes translated). Eyes that do what only healthy eyes can do—focus. "If your eye is healthy, your whole body is full of light; but if it is not healthy, your body is full of darkness" (Luke 11:34).

Full of darkness. That was a chilling warning to a generation that wasn't recognizing him even though he was right in front of them. And it should chill us as well.

So let us, again and again, find ourselves drawn to stare at holy Jesus. And let us, again and again, call our communities of faith to stare at him. Let us be people who honor Jesus by lifting him up constantly, being perennially impressed by him. Let us keep his name close to our lips. Which all brings me to another question for us to chew on.

POTENTIALLY DANGEROUS QUESTION 3: *Is it possible to focus on Jesus too much?*

Quite a question, huh? Is it possible to focus on Jesus too much? On our deathbeds, will we say, "I wish I had spent less time looking at the life of Jesus"? I am sure there are many things that occupy us now that we will one day look back upon and regret spending so much time on. But after considering this question for some time, I don't believe we'll regret a single moment of considering Jesus.

I don't think we can ever be too centered upon Jesus, the one in whose life we see our invisible God revealed. After all, the entire Old Testament gazes ahead, pointing to Jesus. The Acts of the Apostles and the Epistles are Jesus saturated, looking back upon him, echoing him. But Jesus is the point. He is the center. He is the very flesh of invisible God. How could we ever focus on him too much?

I think that the more we see this holy, strange man, the more we will wear out those four Gospel books of our Bibles. And the more we just might spread his fame through our unity.

ELUSIVE UNITY

A beautiful thing happens when we focus on Jesus. We become more unified.

When I stare at Jesus and am amazed, I find growing within me a sense (a real, tangible feeling) of union with others who are also standing, amazed by Jesus. I may not agree with all of your theology, I may be shocked by your views on baptism, I may disagree with what you put in your Communion cup, I may even be offended by your church building, but if you, too, are utterly impressed by Jesus, it changes how I feel about you. Your affection for Jesus makes me want to . . . well, give you a high-five or hug you or worship together or something.

As we each focus on the person of Jesus, we are brought together. The "details" (as significant and important to deal with as they are) shrink in significance when the presence of Jesus looms. And we find ourselves more unified.

This has always been the case with Jesus. Consider the great variety of people who were in the early church and found unity in Jesus. Consider the disciples. A timid Thomas and a fiery Peter. A taxman puppet of the Romans and a revolutionary wanting to violently overthrow the Romans. Disciples who wanted to sit at Jesus' right and left hands and who argued over who was the greatest.

And then consider how the Acts community, this crosscultural, multinational group of believers who had the sometimes jostling disciples as their leaders, was described this way: "Now the whole group of those who believed were of one heart and soul" (Acts 4:32).

One heart and soul! How did they do it? How did they not only endure each other but ultimately find deep, purposeful union and community together? Accounts of the early church in Acts often make modern Christians pine for such union and agreement and purpose and sacrifice. But how often do we stop to recognize that those who made up such a community were formerly sworn enemies?

Did Jesus teach courses on tolerance and hold sensitivity workshops on the weekends for his disciples? Nope. He just was. Was holy and intense and amazing. This riveted his disciples, and they eventually found themselves looking at him and not at their petty disputes as much. Paul celebrates in Galatians that there is no longer Jew or Gentile, male or female, because we each are "clothed" with Jesus (Galatians 3:26-27). So when we look at each other, we see him.

Interestingly, even Jesus' enemies were so taken with his presence that he unified them too. Consider the Pharisees and Herodians. Both powerful schools of thought and seats of political power. Enemies. Rivals. They disagreed on so many issues. Loudly. But then Jesus rolled into town and they became so riveted upon him that their differences were no longer the most important issue. In the pages of the Gospels we find them sitting down together to plot Jesus' death.

Even warring packs of dogs will band together when a lion walks into town. And so it was with Jesus. His holy presence was striking. And as people stared at him, they grew unified.

I once directed a weeklong summer camp for elementary-age kids from Denver. We loaded up eighty kids from the city in huge yellow buses and headed off for a week of chaos in the beautiful Rocky Mountains. It was a great week, but *chaos* really is an apt word for it. Fighting, laughing, screaming, whining, singing—it doesn't matter what time of day, kids of this age, in large quantities, are beautifully loud and energetic and combative.

I'll never forget the afternoon a brown bear lumbered into camp. We were just finishing lunch in the second-story cafeteria and loudly spilling out onto the huge deck that overlooked the whole property. In the midst of this chaos one little girl standing near the railing suddenly stood still and pointed. Her small finger led the eyes of those nearest her (and eventually everyone's eyes) to a young brown bear meandering toward our building.

There was no panic, because we were all up on the second story and the stairs were far on the other side of the building. No panic, but I have never heard such silence. Every kid there stood quiet, curious, entranced side by side on the deck. The racial slurs, the loud flirting, the macho posturing, the arguments that began over lunch all faded away in the presence of such a creature.

This bear was holy, set apart from all we had experienced. It's sheer *otherness* (remember, these were city kids who had rarely if ever come into the mountains) took over camp, and all petty disputes (however valid or silly) took a back seat to staring at this amazing, strange, unpredictable creature. We were one for those moments.

And so it is with Jesus.

Inasmuch as we focus on Jesus, we will find unity as believers. We won't perfectly get along, we won't agree on every issue, we won't disband all denominations and form one church universal in name. But we will attain this seemingly vaporous quantity called unity. Jesus' loudest and longest prayer for his church was for unity (John 17). And yet most of us don't feel unified. Even when we try to grab hold of it, to program in some unity with an ecumenical service or two, it never sticks, never affects our hearts.

How can you program unity, after all? You can't. And inasmuch as Jesus' church continues to be focused on the relative minutiae of our theologies instead of Jesus, we never will attain this blessed state of unity. And according to Jesus, that will continue to make our witness in this world impotent. The world is to know us by our unity (John 17:21). Without unity, or with only token unity exercises from time to time, the world will not know us.

They will continue to laugh at a religion that preaches love while throwing punches. Our hypocrisy condemns us and evangelistically castrates us. We stand, impotent, clutching our petty disagreements and minor theologies. We're angry and defensive. Our Christian radio talk shows are filled with nasty infighting, and personally, many of our thoughts about other churches are laced with jealousy, suspicion and superiority.

All this while Jesus, the Holy, the Other, the Shocking One, sits quietly in our Gospels, used only for Sunday school classes to entertain our children.

Oh, for a church that would think on Jesus. Stare at him. Be amazed by his life. Oh, that we would all major in Jesus and nothing else. That we would find our jaws gaping at Jesus and that when we look at each other, the first thing we would notice would be each other's gaping jaws.

Oh, that such gaping jaws would make us smile and laugh and high-five each other out of the sheer joy of this crazy Jesus.

Oh, that amazement would seize us and we would shake our heads, slap our knees and say to one another, "We have seen strange things today."

Chapter Four
They Worshiped Him

When you spend time walking among the lesser verses, these sometimes-neglected descriptions of how folks responded to Jesus, you end up seeing a lot of church. Yeah, church.

There's no other way to put it: some folks just found worship gushing from their mouths and hands and toes and lips and tongues when they were with Jesus. They didn't thank Jesus. They didn't give him gifts. They didn't ask him questions or seek to follow after him. They simply worshiped. They had church right then and there in plain daylight.

> *Those in the boat worshiped him, saying, "Truly you are the Son of God."* (Matthew 14:33)

> *They came to him, took hold of his feet, and worshiped him.* (Matthew 28:9)

> *When they saw him, they worshiped him.* (Matthew 28:17)

> *They worshiped him, and returned to Jerusalem with great joy; and they were continually in the temple blessing God.* (Luke 24:52-53)

He said, "Lord, I believe." And he worshiped him. (John 9:38)

Fear seized all of them; and they glorified God. (Luke 7:16)

Amazement seized all of them, and they glorified God. (Luke 5:26)

When he laid his hands on her, immediately she stood up straight and began praising God. (Luke 13:13)

Immediately he regained his sight and followed him, glorifying God; and all the people, when they saw it, praised God. (Luke 18:43)

The whole multitude of disciples began to praise God joyfully with a loud voice. (Luke 19:37)

When the centurion saw what had taken place, he praised God. (Luke 23:47)

Some of these folks had just gotten through being healed. That could explain some of their responses. But others (sometimes whole groups of people) were just responding to Jesus himself. Being near him moved them to praise him.

Now, I am assuming that having church on the street corner, by yourself, was as awkward back then as I can imagine it being today. Especially if it was another person that you were worshiping. Especially if it was some blue-collar worker dressed like everyone else, or perhaps more poorly than everyone else, that you were worshiping. So what do we make of this spontaneous praise? And what, if anything, does this teach us about Jesus?

SINGING ROCKS

Let's focus in on that one verse from Luke 19. What does this occasion of spontaneous worship teach us about Jesus? Remember, this is Jesus' last human entry into the big city, Jerusalem. He gets on a colt and rides up the hill into town. But as Luke records it, "the whole multitude of the disciples began to praise God joyfully with a loud voice for all the deeds of power that they had seen" (Luke 19:37).

Perhaps it was the sight of Jerusalem rising before them that loosened their tongues. Perhaps it was the proximity to the temple during festival time that aroused such feeling and joy. But Luke tells us plainly that they started to loudly and joyfully have church because of all the stuff they had seen Jesus do. His works, his divinity were so palpable to them that they rang out in worship.

They sang out songs from their hymnal that were now being realized. Psalm 118 was one they sang:

> Blessed is the King
>> who comes in the name of the Lord!
> Peace in heaven,
>> and glory in the highest heaven! (Luke 19:38)

What a scene! The *whole* multitude of the disciples—the gruff fishermen, the tax collectors, the zealot, even the betrayer, perhaps—all together losing it on their way into the city. Now, this was festival time, so there were lots of folks going up into the city for the celebration. And singing psalms (such as Psalm 118) would have been normal for the day. But something was different here. Very different. And people knew it.

This ragtag group of disciples were not praising God merely as custom for the festival. They were not melting into praise of Yahweh because they were drawing near to his holy temple. No. They were worshiping because of "all the deeds of power that they had seen" (Luke 19:37). They were worshiping because it was Jesus

who had done all those deeds of power and this made them realize that God himself was there in the street next to them. Jesus
smelled of Yahweh and they were overcome with his presence.
Remember that truth proclaimed in Hebrews, "[The Son] is the
reflection of God's glory and the exact imprint of God's very being" (Hebrews 1:3)? If that's really true, it shouldn't surprise us
that they worshiped that day; it should surprise us that it didn't
happen more often!

After all, the disciples were used to a geographically stable
God. Sure, they had studied all about the old tabernacle, how the
Israelites had carried the presence of God around with them. But
for their whole lives Yahweh had dwelt within the holy of holies,
deep within the temple walls in Jerusalem. Thus the temple took
on an immense presence in their lives and thoughts and devotions. And so what a profound shift, what a revolutionary step
when they realized (on the way up to the temple that day) that
God had become portable.

Yahweh was riding a donkey. Right next to them.

And this presence, which their people had alternately feared
and longed to be near for generations, was at hand. God at hand.
The title of one old hymn puts it nicely, "God and Man at Table
Are Sat Down." Indeed. And so they worshiped.

The Pharisees saw it and were outraged and offended. They
called out to Jesus (which, given the singing all around Jesus,
must have taken quite some doing!). They called out to him,
"Teacher, order your disciples to stop" (Luke 19:39). It was just
too much. To worship a mere man? A carpenter? To sing psalms
as if they were being lived out before them? Their anger and dis-
belief poured out, "Rebuke your disciples, Jesus! Put an end to
this farce!"

Farce? Put an end to this spontaneous worship that his divine
presence drew forth from their lips? "Order" the joyful, loud

singing to end? I wonder if Jesus smiled. Or grinned. There must have been a twinkle in his eye as he gave his response to the Pharisees: "I tell you, if these were silent, the stones would shout out" (Luke 19:40).

His presence calls forth worship. Of course these men found church dancing out of their throats. Of course they were singing psalms. If they didn't, the stones themselves, the road they were riding on, would shout out. Even the stones in the road felt his divine presence! The very breath of God, the image of the invisible God, the presence that had filled the holy of holies for centuries was there. In their midst. Worship had to happen.

And so it did.

And it wasn't just this one time that this happened, either. Jesus' divinity, his Godness, struck many he came into contact with. And they just up and worshiped. This response is recorded throughout the Gospels. And we never see any folded bulletins or Sunday-go-to-meeting clothes or organs to get them in the mood. They just praised God. Joyfully.

This was a chance for pure worship, after all: no in-between priests, no hierarchical temple structure, no need to wrack the brain to remember the good deeds of God. No. He was right there in front of them.

God was near and touchable.

But streets were not the appropriate place to worship in those days. And dusty carpenters have never been the right object of worship. So these impromptu outbursts must have caused quite a commotion. If the Pharisees' reaction in Luke 19 is any indication, these spontaneous, beautiful interactions with Jesus were not socially (or theologically) acceptable. At all.

So the people must have been strongly overcome by their desire to worship in order to break the kinds of social and religious rules they broke. Their public worship reminds me of sporting events and baggage claim areas these days.

Most of us know what it's like to be at our favorite team's arena and get to see them live. The rush that comes over you when they first come out into the lights and you realize that you are in the same room as your favorite players. Sure, it's a big room, but you are in it with them! And you just yell and yell and yell . . .

Maybe a concert is more your cup of tea.

My wife once went to a Britney Spears concert and came back with little hearing left in her ears and sobered about the concept of worship. Many of us (no matter how shy or staid we normally are) would immediately let loose if we got to see some of our favorite performers in person. Without even thinking, we might start yelling. Their mere presence would bring that response out of us.

But arenas and stadiums aren't the greatest analogy for what we see in the pages of the Gospels. It's acceptable to yell in a stadium, after all. Expected, even. And at most concerts you can't even hear your own screams because of the deafening roar all around you. So you're not having to overcome any social boundaries at all.

For that reason I think the baggage claim area of any airport may be a bit better parallel.

Coming back from a recent trip, I walked off my plane and slowly made my way (nearly sleepwalking) to my baggage carousel along with the rest of the drowsy crowd. We all stood, silent and professional, waiting for our bags to come slowly across the conveyer belt. The only sound was the faint hum of the engines powering the conveyer belts, the quiet chatter of cell phone users and the occasional, unintelligible announcements coming from the speakers overhead. And that's when it happened.

I was roused from my drowsy half sleep by a piercing scream

of joy. Then another, deeper shout of joy. We all turned our heads, suddenly wide-awake, to see what could be the matter. Right there in our midst a woman ran through the crowd (bumping a few surprised professionals, I might add) and jumped into the arms of what was apparently her man. He held her tight, spinning her in circles, and the two of them (all within arms' reach of the rest of the silent crowd) began kissing and speaking loudly of their love for each other. Right there in the baggage claim area.

Their embrace stayed PG, mostly, so everyone eventually turned away. But that image has stuck with me. What would it take for me to speak out loud in a quiet, professional crowd like that? Let alone run or scream or call out loud about my deepest affections? It would take something pretty special. Or some*one* pretty special, more to the point.

And that's what happened around Jesus again and again. People cried out praises not only at inappropriate times but also to a person they could have been stoned for praising. And yet they did it. What a striking image! No wonder these black verses were recorded. They record something of great significance. And they teach us quite a bit about Jesus.

There was something in his presence that made people disregard social customs by praising right there in the street. There was something in him that made them even risk being accused of heresy.

In Jesus they saw God himself. And found themselves overwhelmed with his divine presence.

PRAISE HIM

What do you do with the divine? With a Savior whose presence has all the closeness of humanity yet retains full divinity? Well, there's not much to say here. You worship. God's presence in

Jesus calls forth worship from us. We can't help but give him glory, sing of his fame, chant about how cool he is.

We praise him. This is our eternal destiny, after all: to yell about how cool God is. One day every knee will bow and every tongue will confess, right? And when we praise him now, when we sing about how cool and different and amazing he is, we are practicing. We are actually getting to speak words upon this earth that have no shadows about them. What a rare treat that is! When we praise, we speak utter truth. We breathe reality.

So let us, too, have church. Let us sing of Jesus' worth. Let us so open our eyes to the presence of the living God in Jesus (who now abides within us) that our throats start to hum and our hips start to sway and a smile just leaps from our usually sober faces.

Sounds simple enough, huh?

So why is it so hard? Why do we have such a tough time allowing ourselves to let go and proclaim publicly our love for God? Why is it so hard to get out of our heads and into our bodies and hearts? We know it's not a given that spontaneous worship will happen, after all. Many people in Jesus' day interacted with him but didn't worship at all. So what was the difference between those who did and those who did not worship Jesus? And what does that speak to us today?

Let's consider some worship that happened in a boat on the Sea of Galilee (Matthew 14:22-33). In this instance the disciples witness Jesus walking on the water before getting in a boat. They are astounded. What happens then? "Those in the boat worshiped him, saying, 'Truly you are the Son of God.' "

Now, these disciples had been with Jesus plenty. They had been in this very boat with him before. They had witnessed him performing miracles on this very lake. But there was something on this evening that made them worship when he got into the boat with them. Something changed when they saw him walking on the water. Their eyes were opened and they realized anew exactly who was getting into the boat with them. Yahweh enfleshed was in their boat. Clarity about his divinity, combined with his close presence among them, was the spark for the worship that came out of them that night.

If you're anything like me, you probably take God's presence for granted a bit. "Jesus in my heart" has become a cliché. A given. A starting place for Sunday school kids to understand the faith. And yet what intense, epic, dripping-with-meaning truth are we closing our eyes and hearts to when we take God's presence for granted? Which brings me to a loaded grenade of a question that I want to lob into our lives.

POTENTIALLY DANGEROUS QUESTION 4: *Is it really Yahweh who lives inside me?*

I mean, really. The Spirit of Jesus that has made a home within me—is it the real presence of fiery, jealous, powerful, divine Yahweh? Or is it a cute, lesser, diminished part of the Trinity?

While my trinitarian beliefs do (mostly) stand up to such questioning, it does something to contemplate this presence of God within me. It allows my heart to enter into mystery. The mystery of the unfathomable presence of the divine within little old me. The mystery of God, who is enthroned right now somewhere in creation, who even now has angels before him singing without ceasing,

> Holy, holy, holy,
> the Lord God the Almighty,
> who was and is and is to come (Revelation 4:8)

—it is his own spirit and presence inside me. The angels worship him. And he also dwells inside me. That's a mystery.

To be honest, it's hard to even ask this question without feeling trite or simple or overly spiritual. But contemplating Jesus' divinity by asking this question and by looking at how people worshiped him in his own day is important.

It's important because it clarifies his divinity. It helps us see him more truly and clearly. And that's of the utmost importance. After all, it was contemplating this divine but near presence of Jesus that caused those disciples on the way up to Jerusalem to lose it that morning. God was at hand. And they knew it.

Perhaps we, too, can join the long list of folks from the Gospels who found themselves having church in broad daylight.

ELUSIVE WORSHIP

We're told that the disciples called out "joyfully with a loud voice" on that road trip up to Jerusalem (Luke 19:37). Those are interesting details to be recorded. Their praise to Jesus wasn't just any old praise. It was joyful. And it was loud. These seemingly insignificant details take us to the crux of what is so elusive in worship, don't they?

Of course genuine worship can easily be silent or quiet. But anyone who has led worship knows what it means to long for people's souls to be free. Not just free to worship in stillness (which makes us cross very few social boundaries) but free to worship loudly and joyfully. Free to acknowledge God without inhibition.

And we know what it is like to be frustrated at the still masses as they painfully, stiffly sing songs about "dancing like David danced." We know deeply the irony of those times. And we know what it's like to try to persuade or cajole or exhort them to really let go and sing as if they meant it. As if God really were big and worthy and at hand.

So we dim the lights and soften our voices. We close our

eyes tight and try to help the congregation along, try to nudge them away from social inhibition and toward a recognition of the divine, of the spiritual realities they sing of. We increase the volume, hoping to elicit more praise, more emotion, more . . . anything.

But even when the crowds respond to our exhortations, even when they take it up a notch, there's something missing. Something flat. Experience this enough times and you know what it is to let go and realize that true worship flows from within, that nothing you do with lighting or instruments or overheads can elicit true, genuine worship.

"Joyfully with a loud voice." In today's world of plugged-in worship and large speakers in nearly every church, we may be able to approximate or fabricate the "loud" part. But joyful? That's harder. There's no knob on the mixing board marked "joy." Unfortunately.

And thus is the elusiveness of worship. It can't be grabbed. Can't (really) be programmed in. It must flow from within. It comes only from seeing Jesus more clearly, from smelling the scent of divinity up close.

Oh, that we would be more open to the mystery of God's presence, that we would contemplate the divine that is at hand in Jesus. Oh, may we find ourselves, like so many people in Jesus' own day, taken by the divine in his presence. Overwhelmed by the scent of Yahweh.

Oh, for a day when we open our eyes wide enough to see God in Jesus.

Oh, for a time when seeing Jesus makes our inhibitions fade away and we find ourselves joyfully singing with the choir of all creation. This choir that's made up of the deepest parts in all of creation (even the stones on the road, apparently) longing to yell out the truth about God. About how cool he is. About our love for him.

Oh, for a church that is loud and joyful again.

Book Three
The Authority of Jesus

Many people (after initially being stunned by Jesus' presence) found in him an authority that spoke to their depths. Some were astounded by his teachings. Others fell in the dirt at his feet.

Was Jesus really that impressive? And what can we learn from those who were so humbled by him?

Chapter Five
They Became Silent

Words are everywhere these days. Our marketplace of ideas has become something of a flea market. With the World Wide Web, pretty much anyone can write and upload anything they want and have a few random hits on their site and be seen as clever. Turning a few heads with some thought or idea or teaching is banal. Not a great accomplishment.

But what does it say if whole crowds are amazed by someone's words? What does it mean if folks are willing to run around a lake and go without food just to hear someone tell stories? What's the significance of a man's enemies (who are professional lawyers!) finding themselves mute before his simple teaching?

With those kinds of responses, we must be talking about a pretty special teacher with some pretty extraordinary words. Consider the effect Jesus' words had on those who heard them.

> *All who heard him were amazed at his understanding and his answers. When his parents saw him they were astonished.* (Luke 2:47-48)

> *Now when Jesus had finished saying these things, the crowds were astounded at his teaching.* (Matthew 7:28)

He came to his hometown and began to teach the people in their synagogue, so that they were astounded and said, "Where did this man get this wisdom?" (Matthew 13:54)

When the crowd heard it, they were astounded at his teaching. (Matthew 22:33)

They were astounded at his teaching, for he taught them as one having authority, and not as the scribes. (Mark 1:22)

They were all amazed, and they kept on asking one another, "What is this? A new teaching." (Mark 1:27)

On the sabbath he began to teach in the synagogue, and many who heard him were astounded. They said, "Where did this man get all this? What is this wisdom that has been given to him?" (Mark 6:2)

They were afraid of him, because the whole crowd was spellbound by his teaching. (Mark 11:18)

He began to teach in their synagogues and was praised by everyone. (Luke 4:15)

All spoke well of him and were amazed at the gracious words that came from his mouth. (Luke 4:22)

They were astounded at his teaching, because he spoke with authority. (Luke 4:32)

They were not able in the presence of the people to trap him by what he said; and being amazed by his answer, they became silent. (Luke 20:26)

About the middle of the festival Jesus went up into the temple and began to teach. The Jews were astonished at it, saying, "How does this man have such learning, when he has never been taught?" (John 7:14-15)

Anyone else notice a theme here? Striking, isn't it? But what does it all mean? Why were people so astounded at his words? And what does this chorus of astonishment teach us about Jesus?

JERUSALEM CAGE MATCH

Let's explore Jesus' last trip into Jerusalem. As Jesus enters the town and begins to teach (a moment the whole country has been waiting for), he is met by a tag team of debaters and lawyers and spies sent to trip him up. I call it the Jerusalem Cage Match.

No holds barred. Large crowds watching. And the best minds and debaters and lawyers of the day licking their chops, waiting for their turn to embarrass this popular, upstart carpenter-turned-religious-teacher in front of all of Jerusalem.

While the arguments that take place are beautiful to study individually (check out all of Luke 20—watching Jesus in action is thrilling!), it's interesting even to follow the end responses of those who are trying to trip him up. Their final words in each debate tell us a lot about Jesus, especially considering their aggressive, cocky posture coming into the debates.

First come a group of chief priests and scribes and elders. Learned men. The elite. They come up to Jesus as a group and question him about his authority. It's a nice trap. They must have been pleased with themselves, thrilled after setting Jesus up for a fall in front of the whole crowd. Yet Jesus, with a few words and a question of his own, has this crew of finely tuned minds reeling. Panicked, they huddle: "What should we say? There's no way out of this!"

And (in front of the crowd they had hoped to humble Jesus in front of) they tell Jesus, "We don't know." We don't know. The last thing you ever want to utter in a public debate comes grudgingly but surely to their lips. *We don't know.*

Not how they wanted this to go. The text tells us that this first group wanted to kill Jesus after watching their clever trap disintegrate (academics can be so insecure!), but instead they "watched him and sent spies who pretended to be honest, in order to trap him by what he said" (Luke 20:20).

In come the spies with their clever trap. This time it's about taxes. But then Jesus responds and we get to the interesting conclusion: "And they were not able in the presence of the people to trap him by what he said; and being amazed by his answer, they became silent" (Luke 20:26). Amazed by his answer. Did you catch that? Clever, subtle, wordsmithing spies, who were sent to "play honest" and then trap Jesus, fell silent before his words. Wow!

But the cage match wasn't over. Next it was the Sadducees' turn. Another clever question. Another response from Jesus. And another, very telling black verse after all was said and done: "Then some of the scribes answered, 'Teacher, you have spoken well.' For they no longer dared to ask him another question" (Luke 20:39-40).

And thus the Jerusalem Cage Match ended. Those who wanted to embarrass and trip up Jesus found themselves silenced. Embarrassed. Tripped up.

This was no plain carpenter. These responses to Jesus tell us, with utter clarity and surety, that when Jesus taught, something amazing was taking place. Every time he opened his mouth, his brilliance and genius came out, simply and easily. But perhaps that shouldn't be too surprising.

THE LIPS OF LOGOS

John tells us that Jesus was the Word become flesh.

We considered in an earlier chapter, "Word" (or *logos* in Greek) means truth or reason or logic or reality. And John tells us that this ultimate expression of truth slipped skin on and became Jesus. So Jesus *was* truth. He *was* logic. He *was* reality.

Ultimately *logos* isn't about ideas. It's about reality—what is. And reality, of course, is the truest thing around. It defines truth. Mere ideas try to peck and scratch at reality, trying to voice an idea that resonates somewhat with reality. But Jesus had nothing to do with these little ideas. His words weren't clever ideas, they were the very breath of reality.

No wonder his words rang within the human soul like no other words ever had. No wonder the people were stunned when he began to teach. No wonder it seemed like nothing they had ever heard before. No wonder they were silenced. No wonder he won the Jerusalem Cage Match with only a few words.

The most cleverly laid theological trap came apart before Jesus. The most unfair, contrived, pointed question fell silent and limp at one word from Jesus. After a while his opponents stopped trying to debate him. With a simple story Jesus could unseat the proudest debaters of his day. With one image Jesus could name, with utter precision and efficiency, a truth of human existence that until that moment had seemed to all around him a tangled mess.

Jesus' words aren't close to the actual words of God—they *are* the actual words of God. According to Jesus, "I have not spoken on my own, but the Father who sent me has himself given me a commandment about what to say and what to speak. . . . What I speak, therefore, I speak just as the Father has told me" (John 12:49-50).

No wonder his words packed so much power. Jesus said his words were like seeds. Little, innocuous, innocent-looking things that, once planted, grow exponentially.

Much of what God told Jesus to speak were seemingly benign

parables. Little stories about sheep and manure and parties. But Jesus used image and metaphor and story like the sharpest of knives. His theology soared to heights upon the wings of simple words. There was no trickery. No obfuscating. No need to rely on intricate sentences to dazzle and confuse and impress his listeners. He had the simple bread of truth and needed no contrived human condiments to spice it up.

God had come enfleshed in Jesus to speak what prophets and kings and angels longed to hear. He sowed explosive seeds that were looking for some good soil. The good Samaritan is not a quaint moral story for kids. It is the sharpest of knives flung strongly by Jesus. It is a theological nuclear bomb, a philosophical land mine—all wrapped up tidily in this simple story. The more you handle the story, the more you get cut and encouraged and challenged and enlightened and humbled.

"Indeed, the word of God is living and active, sharper than any two-edged sword, piercing until it divides soul from spirit, joints from marrow; it is able to judge the thoughts and intentions of the heart" (Hebrews 4:12). Every teaching that Jesus ever spoke is the word of God. And is sharp and alive. Even today.

Jesus' parables are Hebrew, not Greek. The Hebrews had no concept of intellectual belief separate from participation with the whole of life. The Greeks did. The Greeks—so philosophical, so removed, so proud of their lofty ideas—cleverly batted around concepts from a distance, untouched, unscathed, uninvolved. Jesus was not like the Greeks. His teachings were Hebrew: they demanded participation, action, anger—anything!—on the part of the listener.

Jesus knew the nature of truth. That mere ideas are not truth. That reality is truth. And getting humans to step into this realm of reality with their minds and thoughts and hearts and fears and hopes and joys was the real path to truth. This is why he sowed seeds of reality, not mere ideas or concepts. This is why Jesus ended a teaching with the simple but crucial phrase: "Go and do likewise."

Remember Jesus' response to the lawyer who wanted to debate, discuss the law and talk theory (Luke 10:25-37)? Instead of playing that man's sophisticated game, Jesus answered him with a kindergarten lesson about the law, a seemingly simple story and that one, chilling, brilliant phrase: "Go and do likewise."

STUDY HIM

What do you do with a brilliant Jesus? With a Jesus who sows seeds of reality? Not just good ideas or suggestions or clever concepts, but reality. Ultimate truth and reason and clarity and brilliance. What do you do with such a Jesus?

Well, for starters, we could sit at the feet of Jesus and listen. Just listen. The one needful thing that the younger sister Mary knew to do instinctively (Luke 10:38-42). The only thing we really need. Let us read his words. Let us study his teachings. Let us take from the feast of reality and truth he sets before us and have our fill. Let us pore over his parables and images and stories and lessons and appropriate them into our lives.

We often claim to "wrestle" with a passage of Scripture. But doesn't our wrestling usually end with us claiming victory over the text? We "pin" a passage, getting it to stroke our preexisting assumptions. Why not just lay down our assumptions and submit ourselves again and again to Jesus' words? And let them pin us.

Let us major in Jesus' teachings, then. And submit all to them.

Sounds great, right? So why don't we study Jesus and submit to his words more often? If Jesus really is so brilliant, then why do we hesitate to submit to his teachings? I think it's because, when it comes right down to it, we just don't like what he's teaching.

After teaching his disciples one day, Jesus asked them: "Why do you call me 'Lord, Lord,' and do not do what I tell you?" (Luke 6:46). It's an important question because I believe it has an answer.

Why do we do that? Why hear words from the lips of Logos and yet not submit ourselves to them? Well, when you study the beginning of Luke 6, you get an idea of why. You see, Jesus is asking his question at the end of a time of teaching. And when you back up and look at all he had just taught the people, the answer to his question becomes as plain as rain: Why do we not do what you tell us, Jesus? Well, have you been listening to what you've been saying? All your teaching is upside down and nonsensical and weird.

We call you "Lord, Lord" and do not do what you tell us because you tell us to do *such strange things.*

Consider a few of his teachings there in Luke 6: The poor are lucky. The rich are unfortunate. Congratulations to those who mourn today. Give to everyone who begs from you. Bless those who curse you. Do for others what you would want them to do for you . . . And that's just a sampling.

Why do we not do what Jesus tells us? Because (when we're perfectly honest) our common sense makes more sense to us than the words of Jesus. His teachings may be well intentioned and inspirational, but it doesn't seem like they would really hold in everyday life.

"Blessed are you who are poor" sounds sort of nice and spiritual, but when it comes right down to it, it's really the rich whom we think are lucky. "Give to everyone who begs from you" is inspirational talk, but it's overly simplistic and doesn't really work on the streets of our broken cities. "Do to others as you would have them do to you" is admirable sounding, but when I'm really honest about what I want done to me (lots of gifts, surprise parties, regular encouragement, care about my needs, a ready ear to listen to me), I realize what an impossibly high standard of love this is.

Why do we call you "Lord, Lord" but not do what you tell us to do? Because when we're really honest, we have to admit that you sound genuine, but what you tell us to do is just undoable. It will destroy our lives. It's not good advice, Jesus.

This may all sound really harsh, but when I'm honest, I have to admit that this is what I've thought about Luke 6 and the rest of Jesus' more strange teachings for most of my life.

I distinctly remember the first time I realized that Jesus' weird advice in Luke 6 wasn't just inspirational and spiritual sounding but genius. It was a Christmas morning several years ago, and I was sprinting through the snow on an icy road leading to a prison in Ontario, Oregon.

You see, I had been reading Luke 6, and that part about doing to others had caught my attention. I felt vaguely warmed by this teaching. There was something poetic in it, I remember thinking. It sounded so religious and memorable that I had begun to reflect on it and be haunted by it.

At that time my brother was in prison at Snake River Correctional Institute in eastern Oregon, and I knew he was going to be alone all during the holidays. I figured that if I were in prison, I would want family to visit *me* on Christmas. "Do unto others as you would have them do unto you"—it was kind of staring me in the face. So I went. I didn't tell him I was going because . . . well, *I* would want to be surprised if *I* were in prison at Christmas. *Do unto others,* after all.

I didn't have a car, so I took a Greyhound bus (always an adventure) from Tacoma, Washington, to Ontario, Oregon. It was late on a dark and windy Christmas Eve when the bus screeched to a stop in "downtown" Ontario. I trudged through the snow

and ice to the edge of town and got a room in a dingy motel next
to the interstate.

Early Christmas morning (way before the sun even thought
about coming out) I woke up, put on every stitch of clothing I
had brought with me, and left behind my warm motel room to
greet the dark, snow-swept plains of eastern Oregon. Six miles to
the prison: four miles along the interstate, two miles along a
small road leading over a hill to the prison.

On the way I began to doubt Jesus' teachings. *Do unto others*
. . . Yeah, it sounded nice. Nice material for bathroom plaques
and refrigerator magnets. But it had led me to one of the most
painful, awkward times of my life. As I trudged along the interstate, trying to walk the narrow line between getting run over by
speeding semis on my left and falling down the embankment on
my right, I began daydreaming about that motel room. That
warm, comfy motel room. Had cable, you know. But here I was:
cold, tired, walking along an interstate in the dead dark of morning daydreaming about why sidewalks were never built along interstates.

Do unto others . . . What an upside-down, ludicrous piece of advice, Jesus. I thought about my girlfriend, about her parents who
loved me and had invited me to spend Christmas with them. In
their warm house. Far from any interstates.

But I was roused from my daydreams after taking the small
road that headed from the interstate to the prison when I came
over a small hill and saw the prison (razor wire gleaming in the
rising sun) far off in the distance. Farther than I had thought it'd
be. I looked at my watch and realized I wasn't going to make it on
time. Visiting hours were limited. Get there late, you get less time
to visit.

And something happened then: in my heart I longed to be
there on time. I wanted my brother to get every possible moment

out of his cell on that Christmas day. I longed for that. And so I started to run.

Slowly at first. A few cars would drive by, so I'd slow down and move to the edge of the road. I was self-conscious about running on the road. I was self-conscious about my three layers of clothes and my big army jacket. After the cars passed, I started running again. I checked my watch and began to run faster. Some more cars came by, but I didn't slow down or even give them much room to pass—I was running!

I was just flat-out running. Eyes locked ahead on that prison, straining with everything in me to get there. Something inside my soul had clicked into place—this longing, this deep desire to lay down everything I had to make sure my brother got all his visiting time. I imagined him getting his name called and his cell door sliding open to his surprise. And I ran faster. My lungs began to ache, my legs were getting rubbery, cars were swerving around this weird, army jacket-laden guy who was taking up most of the road. But none of it mattered. All that mattered was getting there for my brother.

And that's when it happened.

As I ran along the road that morning, caring more about my brother getting all of his time than about my tired legs or aching lungs or embarrassing appearance, I felt more human, more alive than I ever had in my life. And I realized that Jesus had been right. That he was a genius.

Jesus was right. *Do unto others . . .* My own common sense never would have gotten me out of that motel room. Well, let's be honest: I never would have left town on a Greyhound on Christmas Eve to begin with! But Jesus' upside-down, ludicrous teaching (which I had seriously started to doubt while trudging along the frozen, unwelcoming interstate) turned out to be right. It was right! I couldn't believe it! *Do unto others . . .* He wasn't just trying to be inspirational—he was being brilliant. It wasn't a clever idea, it was a seed of reality that was only waiting for my heart to be good soil so that it could grow and grow and grow and grow . . .

The rest of the day was a gift from brilliant Jesus. "And these are the ones sown on the good soil: they hear the word and accept it and bear fruit, thirty and sixty and a hundredfold" (Mark 4:20). I got to experience fruit that day because I had submitted to Jesus' seemingly upside-down teaching.

I got to run the remaining mile and arrive breathless. Breathless in my body from having sprinted the last two miles. Breathless in my spirit from the staggering realization that Jesus *had known all along.* He knew that laying my life down would leave me blessed and joyful and feeling truly human. I was shocked at his genius.

I got to have an unforgettable conversation with a very tense, very confused guard (apparently a skinny guy with a bulky army jacket sprinting toward the prison is on the guard's list of "questionable activities"!).

I got to see my brother's shock and surprise when he noticed me sitting at the small white card table in the visiting room. I got to laugh and sing and joke around with him on a bright Christmas morning. I got to talk about life with him and sit, peacefully, as brothers.

When my brother found out that I had walked (and run!) all the way out to the prison, I got to explain why I would give up a comfortable Christmas to run through the snow and visit a brother who had treated me so poorly while growing up. I got to tell him of Jesus and what I had learned that morning about his words.

I got to cry together with my brother that Christmas morning. And laugh. And sing. We filled the awkward air of the stiff prison visiting room with the sounds of heaven on that Christmas day. The looming guards and prison uniforms and razor wire faded away and we sat as brothers. And celebrated Christmas.

My favorite Christmas ever.

Now that day didn't happen because I was loving and clever and nice. Nothing of the sort. That day wasn't my idea. *Do unto others* . . . That day happened because I had dared to submit myself to the words of Jesus. And it turns out he is brilliant. And his words usher us into reality.

Jesus was not a good teacher. Never be confused about that. He didn't teach nice little aphorisms. He didn't come with clever observations and apt suggestions. No. Jesus was *brilliant*. He knew—with utter precision—what leads to life and what doesn't. And it just so happens that the way to life seems a little upside down at first glance. I figure that's why Jesus tells the house-on-a-rock parable at the end of Luke 6.

In Luke 6 Jesus teaches all these weird, upside-down-sounding things. Then he asks the disciples why they call him "Lord, Lord" yet don't do what he tells them to do. (They don't answer, of course, because it would be too harsh to tell Jesus that what he's suggesting is a little too ridiculous and foolhardy.)

Even though they don't answer his question out loud, Jesus speaks, I believe, to their unspoken concerns: "I will show you what someone is like who comes to me, hears my words, and acts on them" (Luke 6:47). He then tells of a solid, sturdy, lasting house. "But the one who hears and does not act is like . . ." (verse 49), and he paints a picture of a tenuous, awkward, fragile, superficial house.

I think Jesus knew that when it comes right down to it, we're tempted to believe that really trusting his strange words will lead to a fragile life and that following common sense will be more secure. And so he sets us straight once and for all: Do these crazy things and you will have life. Ignore my words and live according to your common sense, and your life will be fragile and precarious. This clear teaching of his begs another explosive question for us to detonate within our souls.

POTENTIAL LY DANGEROUS QUESTION 5: *Where do I disagree with Jesus?*

Yeah, disagree. Sit down and study the Gospels until you reach a teaching that makes you feel like Jesus is exaggerating a bit. Overstating things. Getting carried away. It's important that we find those teachings. Because then we can consider what it would mean to dare to believe *him* rather than our own common sense.

His way may *seem* upside down (running in the snow toward a prison on Christmas morning), but it really does lead to having a house built on rock (feeling more human than ever and having an unforgettable, joyful Christmas). Paul reminds us that "God's foolishness is wiser than human wisdom" (1 Corinthians 1:25). The question is this: will we dare to believe in his "foolishness" rather than our own wisdom?

If we would only be honest about our dissonance with brilliant Jesus and be willing to submit to him, we might just find these reality seeds blossoming within our lives. His words aren't meant to be nodded at. They are meant to shock us with their exponential growth and their taste of reality.

ELUSIVE WISDOM

I believe something extraordinary happens when we submit ourselves to Jesus' teaching. We become wise.

Wisdom is a unique quality. It's something we all long for and yet can't produce on our own. It's a beautiful state of being that shows up knowledge and learning and scholarship and expertise for the shallow things they are.

There are no classes or seminars we can take to get wisdom, of course. It can't be grasped by the neck or won like so many other attainable treasures. Anyone with the time and money and inclination can become an expert in theology. Anyone can become biblically literate. Anyone can spend the time and energy to overflow with knowledge.

But we all know what it's like to come upon those who are actually wise. Who not only have knowledge but also have this deeper, more elusive quality that, at once, strikes deep within us and makes us long to learn from them and be near them. More than street smarts, different from common sense, so much more than knowledge, wisdom rests in the soul and body, not content to reside solely in the mind.

And the more we study Jesus, the more we submit ourselves to his teachings, the more of this elusive wisdom we will find clinging to us. It can't be grabbed, but inasmuch as we submit ourselves to Jesus' teachings, it clings to us.

After washing his disciples' feet, Jesus looked around at the shocked room full of his followers and assured them, "If you know these things, you are blessed if you do them" (John 13:17). They could have just taken Jesus' lesson in theory (*Ah yes, he washed our feet. He's saying something about the servant nature of Christ. Very interesting*). But according to Jesus, unless they actually took off their own outer garments, stooped down and busied themselves in humbly washing the feet of their neighbors, they would miss the point. The seed won't have found soil.

Wisdom is won only in such a Hebrew, messy way. We participate with Jesus' teachings with our time and energy and hearts, and thus his seeds can grow exponentially within us. Over time, a life submitted to Jesus begins to smell of reality. And this is what we call wisdom.

Inasmuch as we, his church, continue to play our own games with his teachings, they will seem interesting at best. But inas-

much as we study him intensely and with submission, we will begin to reek of reality.

Let us, then, sit at the feet of his teachings. Let us not stop at
understanding Jesus' work on the cross and his sweet forgiveness. May we also dive with effort into his sublime, seemingly upside-down words and teachings.

Let us fight the temptation to devotionally take a sentence or
two from Jesus out of context and feel satisfied. May we do the
hard work of seeking to understand his teachings in the context
and culture they were spoken in. So that, then, we can breath in
his full, entire breath of reality.

We *could* simply read a sentence like "Come to me, all you that
are weary and are carrying heavy burdens, and I will give you rest"
(Matthew 11:28) and smile and feel like we got a religious hug
from Jesus. But why settle for plucking a sentence out of context
and licking it for the weakened taste that still clings to it, when
we could feast on the meat-and-potatoes meal of his straight
truth by an in-depth study of Matthew 11?

Enough of those well-meaning but disastrous platitude-rid-
den Christian gift books that pluck Jesus' truth out of context
like his teachings are a spiritual salad bar of vague religious say-
ings from which we can pick and choose bite-size morsels. We
need to feast on his words. Dwell in them. Study them. Submit
ourselves to them. Allow them to pin us and transform our
worldview.

———————

Oh, for a time when Jesus' parables are no longer tossed away
to our children like snacks.

Oh, for a time when we will study his parables, when we center
our curriculum on Jesus' words. Oh, for a time when we dare to

believe Jesus' strange teachings rather than politely and respect-fully nodding at them as the naive religious sentiments that we so often take them for.

Oh, for a time when the world stands shocked at the church's wisdom. *Where did they get such wisdom without having studied?* Oh, for a time when the church's wisdom in handling seeming quag-mires (such as racial fighting, profitable oppression, poverty) leave the world stunned. Silent. Wondering where such utter wis-dom could have been won.

All we could do in such a moment is point to Jesus. The bril-liant one. The genius. The true Logos of all reality. And smile.

Chapter Six
They Fell Down Before Him

On a normal day I don't sit on the ground. I just don't.

When I'm camping or hiking, sure. But even then I am care-ful—I'll sit on a rock or log, rather than just plop right down on the dusty trail.

As a culture, we're just not on the ground that often. I grew up in a church where we knelt as part of the liturgy. But even then we had raised kneelers to keep our clothes clean and dignify the whole kneeling process, which, given the whole point of kneel-ing, is perhaps counterproductive.

In this chapter we will see a lot of people on the ground as they respond to Jesus. It's probably the most striking theme, from a visual perspective, to be found within the black verses of the Gospels.

> *Suddenly a leader of the synagogue came in and knelt before him.* (Matthew 9:18)

> *A [Syrophoenician] woman . . . came and bowed down at his feet.* (Mark 7:25)

> *A man ran up and knelt before him.* (Mark 10:17)

There was a man covered with leprosy. When he saw Jesus, he bowed with his face to the ground. (Luke 5:12)

When Mary came where Jesus was and saw him, she knelt at his feet. (John 11:32)

When Jesus said to [the detachment of soldiers and police of the high priest], "I am he," they stepped back and fell to the ground. (John 18:6)

On entering the house, [the wise men from the East] saw the child [Jesus] with Mary his mother; and they knelt down and paid him homage. (Matthew 2:11)

[The Samaritan] prostrated himself at Jesus' feet. (Luke 17:16)

Simon Peter . . . fell down at Jesus' knees, saying, "Go away from me, Lord, for I am a sinful man!" (Luke 5:8)

Whenever the unclean spirits saw him, they fell down before him and shouted, "You are the Son of God!" (Mark 3:11)

When [the demoniac] saw Jesus from a distance, he ran and bowed down before him. (Mark 5:6)

The woman, . . . in fear and trembling, fell down before him. (Mark 5:33)

Now, if only one or two folks fell at Jesus' feet, we could easily dismiss their actions (maybe they were self-deprecating or had tripped) and get on with our study of meaningful themes found within the Gospels. But here we are faced with various people, of various backgrounds, all kneeling at the feet of Jesus. Each Gospel writer felt that this kneeling was significant enough to record. So we can only conclude that this symphony of folks falling at Jesus' feet teaches us something important. And is therefore worth a closer look.

JESUS' DIRTY FEET UP CLOSE

Let's look more closely at one day in the life of Jesus that involved a fair amount of kneeling (Mark 4:35–5:43).

It starts innocently enough: Jesus is teaching by the sea and the crowd grows so large that he needs to get into a boat and push out from shore a bit to address everyone. He teaches all day long. And then evening comes.

He has his disciples head off across the Sea of Galilee. A great storm develops on the lake and the brave, experienced fishermen shake in fear while Jesus sleeps soundly, quietly. They wake him up and, at a word, the sky and sea and wind and waves and clouds obey. We're not even to the real "kneeling" yet, but even here it's almost as if nature itself kneels at his feet. The wind and waves bow down in submission. Obedient, quiet upon his command. "Then the wind ceased, and there was a dead calm" (Mark 4:39).

When they land on the other side of the lake, an enraged, demon-possessed, half-naked man runs straight up to Jesus. This man is all cuts and bruises and muscle and dirt. The townsfolk had tried to chain him, but every bond and chain he would bang and rip and twist until it gave way to his tightly wound arms and hands. He lived in the tombs. He howled like a wolf and hit himself with stones. The townsfolk steered clear and prayed fervently that their children would never get within his terrible reach.

And this man, this tight ball of sinews and muscles and bruises and pain and demonic energy, runs straight at Jesus as he is getting out of the boat. (Imagine the panic on the part of the disciples, the adrenaline rush, the quick, furtive thoughts: *What do I do? Do I try to stop him? Do I pull Jesus back into the boat?*)

But the adrenaline is all for nothing. The demon-possessed, crazed man falls on his knees before Jesus. And begs.

Begs. "What have you to do with me, Jesus, Son of the Most

High God? I adjure you by God, do not torment me" (Mark 5:7). He bows facedown to the ground, shaking, pleading before Jesus. And at a word, the demons give up their prized possession. The man is sane and whole and committed to Jesus, ready to get in the boat and follow him anywhere.

But at another word from Jesus, he denies his strong desire to go with this healer and heads back instead to his hometown to proclaim Jesus' power and authority there. Again, only a word from Jesus and he obeys.

When Jesus and his disciples cross back over the Sea of Galilee, a leader of the synagogue runs up to Jesus. And falls at his feet. And begs. He begs for Jesus to heal his daughter. He, a man of position and power, in broad daylight falls in the dirt before Jesus.

Jesus goes with this ruler, but on the way he is stopped by a woman who touches his cloak. When Jesus stops the crowd and asks who touched him, this poor woman comes and, yes, kneels before him. Falls on her face before him.

Are we starting to notice a theme here? This was the life of Jesus. His authority and rightful lordship emanated from him, and folks, from the demon-possessed to the powerful to the desperate, found themselves at his feet.

Perhaps we could explain away the kneeling of mere outcasts and lepers. But rulers? Close friends? A group of soldiers on a serious mission? Foreign wise men? There must have been something within Jesus that called forth this response. Why else would so many different types of people have this same reaction to him?

Many of these folks had never even met Jesus before. Something just gave way within their souls, and legs, and they could do nothing but fall before him. We have no indication that Jesus ever requested that people kneel before him. He never asked for it. And there was certainly nothing in his poor dress or ragged appearance that would suggest that folks should kneel before him.

(Jesus often critiqued the Pharisees' immature habit of dressing to impress those around him, right?) It must have been something in his very being. But what was it in Jesus that caused all this kneeling?

As we read the larger context of each kneeling incident, we notice that there are real differences. Some are kneeling while begging for a healing from Jesus: "Lord, if you choose, you can make me clean" (Matthew 8:2). Others fall down before him in acknowledgment of who he is: "You are the Son of God" (Matthew 14:32). And others have just witnessed Jesus perform a miracle and are kneeling from thanksgiving or out of fearful, almost embarrassed reverence for this Jesus, who they suddenly realize is more than a simple, poorly dressed teacher: "Go away from me, Lord, for I am a sinful man!" (Luke 5:8).

Different stories, but one obvious commonality: the folks' encounter with Jesus led them to lower themselves, to get in the dirt at his feet. What does that simple, striking decision tell us about these folks and, ultimately, about what it was in Jesus that caused this kind of reaction?

Well, to kneel before someone is embarrassing, humbling. (Try it sometime—you'll see.) It acknowledges relative positions: *My place is low—face in the ground, in fact. Yours is to stand over me.* It is, literally, to put yourself in your place. And thereby acknowledge another's rightful place above you. It is the *definition* of humbling to kneel at the feet of another. It is vulnerable. How do you protect yourself with your face in the dirt? You don't. That's the point of kneeling. You are placing yourself at the will of another.

And you can't really hedge your bets while kneeling. The nature of this physical gesture that we see in the Gospels is that of giving up, giving over your rights and service to another.

If kneeling lowers oneself, it lifts up another. These incidents of kneeling in the dirt at Jesus' feet speak clearly about people's recognition of the place of Jesus—above them. It speaks about the authority that resided within Jesus, as person after person placed him higher than themselves in this graphic, physical act of kneeling before him. There was something about Jesus, an authority that was as real and palpable as that dirt on his sandaled feet.

These kneeling verses clarify for us that Jesus' place is on a throne. He has authority and lordship. He is a Lord. *The* Lord. He may be a merciful, graceful, patient, loving Lord, but let there be no mistake: he is Lord. Our place is at his feet. Humbled. Silent. He may woo people to him as a lover. But he doesn't have to. At his word he could command all attention and obedience. He is Lord over all. That is not just fodder for a worship song—that is reality.

He is Lord over everything. His authority knows no bounds. It extends into every corner of our lives, every moment of our days, every decision we make. There is something in the souls of humans (no matter how deeply hidden) that longs to kneel before the dense, palpable, right authority of Jesus.

FEAR HIM

What do you do with a king?

That may seem an odd question. But it's a good one. Especially these days. We're so accustomed to democracies and committees and consensus decision making and child-centered parenting that we've lost an innate, natural sense of what to do when confronted with authority. Real authority. A King. A Lord. In a world of voting and public polls we need to relearn silent submission. And reverence.

We need to relearn how to kneel.

We need to relearn how to shut our mouths and simply *be* before Jesus. To humbly submit to his authority. We need to start figuring out how to lay aside our penchant for arguing with God, for negotiating with him, for thinking we're pulling the wool over his eyes, for thinking we're doing him favors by obeying him. We need to lay aside all these false, silly games and fall at his feet. And know awe. And submission. And humility. And reverence.

The fear of the Lord was an important Jewish concept. There was no question that God was to be feared, to be revered. These strong, daring nomadic men and women who could brave the wilds of the desert and wilderness wouldn't even dare utter God's name. Let alone write it down. He was too holy, too powerful to regard casually or with haphazard comments.

The Old Testament is ripe with this fear of the Lord. But that doesn't mean this has to be an outdated, antiquated experience. In fact, I recently saw the fear of the Lord in my three-year-old son, Simon.

He had run into our house because a thunderstorm had begun outside. The thunder terrified him. He curled up on the couch with me, and we stared out the window together, Simon's eyes wide and afraid and curious. Then he looked at me and asked, "Where does thunder come from?" A good question, Simon.

How to answer? With science or theology? I chose theology and told him that God made the thunder. His eyes got even wider. He had heard of God before. "Where *is* God?" he asked.

I grinned. Sounds like a simple enough question, doesn't it? I told Simon that God was everywhere: in the clouds, in heaven, outside, in the room with us . . . and Simon shot up! He stared, wide-eyed, looking around the room without blinking. "He's . . . in *here?*"

I caught the connection (loud, scary thunder is made by God, and God is in this room!) and prepared to correct Simon, to calm him and explain that God wouldn't make thunder in the room, that, yes, thunder is loud and scary, but God is calm and nice and

. . . and then I paused. And *I* shot up! The God that could make thunder like that . . . in *my* living room? And instead of calming Simon with the theology of a soft, sedate, suburban God, I was chilled and sobered and humbled by my son's (much more accurate) theology of the fear of the Lord.

Job, like my son Simon, learned what it meant to kneel before the authority of the Lord. Though strong through most of his suffering, Job does question God eventually. God defends his authority with powerful words that sound more than slightly foreign to our democratic ears:

> The LORD answered Job out of the whirlwind:
> "Who is this that darkens counsel by words without
>   knowledge?
> Gird up your loins like a man,
>   I will question you, and you shall declare to me.
>
> "Where were you when I laid the foundation of the earth?
>   Tell me, if you have understanding.
> Who determined its measurements—surely you know!
>   Or who stretched the line upon it?
> On what were its bases sunk,
>   or who laid its cornerstone
> when the morning stars sang together
>   and all the heavenly beings shouted for joy?
>
> "Or who shut in the sea with doors
>   when it burst out from the womb?—
> when I made the clouds its garment,
>   and thick darkness its swaddling band,
> and prescribed bounds for it,
>   and set bars and doors,
> and said, 'Thus far shall you come, and no farther,
>   and here shall your proud waves be stopped'?" (Job 38:1-11)

God goes on. He roars his authority through these questions to Job. And Job kneels. (Seems that's the thing to do around authority.)

> See, I am of small account; what shall I answer you?
>   I lay my hand on my mouth.
> I have spoken once, and I will not answer;
>   twice, but will proceed no further. (Job 40:4-5)

There is a time to go to God like his children with our needs and wants and desires. It is okay to complain, to cajole. God can handle that. He is our very dear, close friend. We know this about him clearly. There are times when casually "hanging" with God is what his Spirit would have for us.

But there is also a time to, in the sober words of Job, "lay our hands on our mouths." To be in silence and submission before God. To fear him.

I wonder sometimes if we have reacted too strongly to the caricature of the Puritans' angry, starched-shirt God and the revivalists' fire-and-damnation gospel. Many people no longer capitalize their divine pronouns, and perhaps for perfectly fine reasons. And many of our modern worship songs sing of a friendly, close, affirming Jesus, which is biblical and wonderful.

But is all of this perhaps a sign that we've swung too far in our theology? That we've forgotten what it is to kneel? What it means to fear the Lord? How to shut up and acknowledge our place? And His? Is it possible that the observation in Psalm 36:1 ("There is no fear of God before their eyes") is relevant today? Perhaps we as a church need to consider another simple but bothersome question.

POTENTIALLY DANGEROUS QUESTION 6: *Did God get smaller when he incarnated?*

Did he get smaller? Did he diminish in authority? Have his authority and dominion shrunk over the years, leaking out of him bit by bit over the centuries? When Jesus walked this earth, did he have all the authority of Yahweh—mighty, jealous, roaring, Creator-of-the-Leviathan Yahweh? And does he still have all that authority today?

Perhaps this is a silly question. But it can definitely help us take steps toward acknowledging what rulers and soldiers and every demon he ever came in contact with knew so plainly: Jesus has authority.

And the more we see Jesus clearly in all his authority, the more we may relearn how to kneel. And how to lay our hands on our mouths.

ELUSIVE HUMILITY

Many of us have contemplated this thing called humility. We've rolled it around in our minds, pondering it: Is humility thinking you are worthless? What of healthy self-love and pride? Does it mean we pretend (in public) not to be as pleased with ourselves as we really are? Feigning ignorance of our own accomplishments and gifts? Is *that* humility?

We've all probably heard variations of the joke that pokes fun at the elusiveness of humility: A woman arrives at the Pearly Gates and is asked about various sins. She replies to each inquiry by saying that she has indeed not committed those sins. At the end of the interview the angel smiles and says, "Well, you haven't committed any of these sins. You must be very proud." The woman smiles and nods . . . and then grimaces, realizing she has fallen into pride!

Or something like that.

Humility is elusive. Many of us have wondered if you can ever really know you're humble. "I am so humble!" seems to be an impossible statement to declare. Saying it disqualifies you. Or even thinking it—doesn't that ruin the whole deal as well?

Thus are our ponderings of this elusive virtue, humility.

And there's no wonder it remains elusive and vaporous, given the culture we live in. Humility is about as un-American a virtue as I can imagine. Can you think of something further from what our culture lifts up and encourages? Of all the personalities we are given as heroes, perhaps only a few demonstrate something akin to humility. What is lifted up before our eyes in this country is vanity. Vanity and presumption and celebrity and arrogance and name-dropping are the air we breathe in this country. No wonder we have a hard time appreciating or recognizing or even *defining* humility.

Other traits masquerade as humility. Self-deprecation, for example, spends a lot of time parading around as humility. But it's just a farce. It's not true humility. Being coy about our successes is not humility. Feigning ignorance of our accomplishments so that others will loudly declare them is not humility.

So what is humility? Well, it has something to do with acknowledging true places. "Poverty of spirit" is a phrase that's gone out of use recently, but it is another wonderful biblical phrase that can help us get a sense of humility. Poverty of spirit is a deep knowledge of how poor and broken our own spirits are.

Those who grow up poor usually only realize their poverty when they see rich people for the first time. Similarly, we can only know our own poverty of spirit when we see that which is truly rich in spirit—Jesus. Poverty of spirit is not a self-deprecation that gets down on oneself. That's a different fruit. Low self-esteem understands that I am low. True humility understands that I am low but that there is something truly high and worthy. True poverty of spirit is marked by a clear vision of how rich and beautiful Jesus is.

Pictures are usually helpful in defining unfamiliar concepts, so let's consider a couple together.

Remember John the Baptist? Wild John. Ate locusts, wore camel hair, lived in the wilderness and had a confrontational, intense ministry to thousands of people. And yet when speaking of Jesus, he had no problem turning to the crowds and saying, "I baptize you with water for repentance, but one who is more powerful than I is coming after me; I am not worthy to carry his sandals" (Matthew 3:11). Not worthy to carry his sandals.

Is John just having an awkward moment? Is he having a bad day and doubting himself a bit? Should we cheer him up and not let him cut himself down like that? No. Of course not. John's assessment that he is not worthy to carry the sandals of Jesus is a correct assessment. He *isn't* worthy. Not because he thinks he is a particularly bad person, but because he knows so clearly how high and full of authority is the one coming after him. John is giving us a picture of true humility.

Or consider the centurion—a soldier and leader who has many people reporting to him. A man of means in his context. And yet this leader of men, when asking Jesus for a healing, declares without missing a beat, "Lord, I am not worthy to have you come under my roof" (Matthew 8:8). Again, we have no reason to believe he was insecure or doubting himself—he talks clearly in the next verses about being a man with authority who commands men and sees them obey. He merely saw himself next to Jesus.

And his conclusion was correct. He *wasn't* worthy to have Jesus in his house. No one was. Jesus later comments that he had never seen faith like the centurion's in all of Israel: a faith that recognized his own poverty of spirit compared to Jesus.

The beautiful thing is that as we are confronted plainly with the authority of Jesus, humility grows within us. Again, it can't be grabbed or faked or programmed in. It can only grow within us. And sitting before the authority of Jesus, kneeling before him

as King, rightly putting our hands upon our mouths—this is the
fertile ground within which it can find root. And grow.

What could a church of humble men and women, a church of
believers closely in touch with the authority of their God, do
upon this earth? How pliable would such a church be in the
hands of the Holy Spirit? There is nothing much more beautiful
in humanity than true, simple humility. What would the world do
with a humble, free church?

And how much more free would we be if we would but fall on
our faces at his feet and know the true poverty of our spirits and
the true beauty of his? The more we grow accustomed to this
true, gospel posture, the more other, false postures will feel
forced and awkward. True humility has a way of making self-deprecation and feigned humility taste sour to the soul.

May the fear of the Lord be understood and embraced again.
And may it cleanse us of the grime that sticks to us in an age of
self-promotion and vanity.

Oh, for a church that acknowledges the Lord's authority. Oh,
that we would find real, tangible humility growing within us.
That our knees would grow more tired than our jaws.

Oh, for a day when we finally understand, with all our beings,
that the poor in spirit are truly blessed, for the kingdom is theirs.

Cleanse us, Jesus. Heal us. Wash away the pride that clings to
us. Help us see you clearly and know, in that glance more than
while glancing in our mirrors, who we really are.

Book Four
The Compassion of Jesus

The four Gospels are full of emotional details. For example, they describe Jesus holding a man's hand, shedding tears for a friend and sighing deeply in his spirit. They also painstakingly describe the anger of Jesus' enemies and show us Jesus getting spit at and slapped and ridiculed.

Why were these details recorded? And why should these vivid descriptions matter to us today?

Chapter Seven
He Touched Her Hand

The Gospels contain a surprising number of references to Jesus' hands. In fact, we're probably told more about Jesus' hands than about the hands of any other religious leader in history. Considering the razor-sharp truths he spoke, considering the powerful deeds he wrought, considering the unquestionable authority he held over people, it is noteworthy—and perhaps spectacular—that such small details were recorded.

And yet in the pages of the Gospels, in the land of the blue-collar verses, we see Jesus' hands again and again. Consider a few examples.

Moved with compassion, Jesus touched their eyes. (Matthew 20:34)

Moved with pity, Jesus stretched out his hand and touched him. (Mark 1:41)

He stretched out his hand and touched him. (Matthew 8:3)

He touched her hand. (Matthew 8:15)

He touched their eyes. (Matthew 9:29)

Jesus came and touched them, saying, "Get up and do not be afraid." (Matthew 17:7)

He took him aside in private, away from the crowd, and put his fingers into his ears, and he spat and touched his tongue. (Mark 7:33)

He took the blind man by the hand and led him out of the village. (Mark 8:23)

Jesus laid his hands on his eyes again. (Mark 8:25)

He came forward and touched the [coffin], and the bearers stood still. (Luke 7:14)

He touched [the soldier's] ear and healed him. (Luke 22:51)

Throughout the Gospels we are shown Jesus' hands as he touches the hurting, as he calms the fearful, as he holds someone's hand gently. This God, this Creator of all, this incarnate Word who could have spoken everything out of existence with one commanding word, this immense, looming Jesus softly held the hand of a blind man. Touched the ears of the deaf. Touched the wasting skin of lepers. Felt the sick eyes of the blind with his fingers.

Why did the Gospel writers record these details? And what do the actions of his hands tell us about Jesus himself?

GENTLE AND HUMBLE IN HEART

Let's consider the story of Jesus and the two blind men. Jesus had just raised someone from the dead, and stories about the resurrection were spreading feverishly throughout the district. As Jesus went along, two blind men heard that he was near and began crying loudly, "Have mercy on us, Son of David!" (Matthew

9:27). They even followed Jesus into a nearby house.

Now, Jesus could have just healed them and gotten on with his agenda. But it would seem they *were* his agenda. It seems he didn't just have healing power but also—as they had asked for explicitly—mercy.

Jesus stopped and asked them, "Do you believe that I am able to do this?" (Matthew 9:28). They did. They told him so. So Jesus touched their eyes. He touched the part of them that was responsible for so much pain and shame in their lives. Jesus touched those eyes with mercy. And they were healed.

Later in Matthew we hear of two more blind men (Matthew 20:29-34). Jesus was again on the road, this time leaving Jericho. Two blind men who were on the roadside to beg heard that Jesus was going past. And they, too, called out to him with loud voices, "Lord, have mercy on us, Son of David!" (verse 30). The crowd grew impatient with these pestering blind men. *Shut up,* they hissed. *Jesus is a busy man!* The crowd sternly ordered them to be quiet. But the two blind men only called out louder and louder, "Lord, have mercy! We need some *mercy* here!"

Jesus heard them and stopped. At this point the narrative slows down. Jesus looks at them. He asks what they want from him. And they answer, "Lord, let our eyes be opened" (Matthew 20:33). Then Matthew records the ending of the story: "Moved with compassion, Jesus touched their eyes" (verse 34). He granted mercy. He paused from the whirl of the crowd and leaned in to these desperate men. He leaned in with compassion. And touched them.

When children were brought to Jesus, the proud disciples turned them away. *Jesus has no time for this!* But Jesus rebuked the disciples, he stopped to hold infants, to play with children, to stroke the wispy hair of a newborn. This jealous God of the Israelites, as it turns out, has gentle hands.

In Mark 7 and 8 we are given two stories of healings. Jesus heals a deaf man with an impediment of speech. And he heals another blind man at Bethsaida. Healing was common enough. But when we pause to ask why Jesus healed the way he did (and why these details were recorded), we are left contemplating the gentle, merciful hands of Jesus.

He starts by taking both men away from the crowds. No show here—it's between Jesus and these men. We're told explicitly that Jesus took the second man's hand in his own to lead him to a private place. He takes them away from the crowds and then heals them with his hands. We know he could have simply willed their health, but he didn't. And there is meaning in that.

There is meaning in the fact that Jesus touched them where they were hurting and broken. It is theologically significant that Jesus took them away from the crowds, that he took time to be with them and heal them. These details clarify that our Jesus is a Jesus of mercy. Any image of Jesus that shows him as lacking compassion and mercy is a false image. The Gospels show us in these important details that he was a man of gentleness.

Instead of setting a blistering pace as a religious reformer, Jesus slowed down to talk with the poor. He could have healed long-distance all the time (it obviously was not hard for him, since he did it on several occasions), but instead of waving his hand over an entire village and creating mass healing, he walked slowly into the heart of a place, stopping to touch the sick. To hold hands. To embrace small babies as their proud mothers looked on.

No wonder the hurting and outcast of his day were so at home with him. Those who needed mercy found it in him. He was not a proud, stiff, religious man. He was sought out by the broken, the outcast, the insulted. He was a "man of sorrows, and acquainted with grief" after all (Isaiah 53:3 RSV). He was utterly, deeply compassionate.

Consider another batch of blue-collar verses recorded in the details of the Gospels.

When he saw the crowds, he had compassion for them, because they were harassed and helpless, like sheep without a shepherd. (Matthew 9:36)

When he went ashore, he saw a great crowd; and he had compassion for them. (Matthew 14:14)

As he came near and saw the city, he wept over it. (Luke 19:41)

Jesus began to weep. (John 11:35)

He was grieved at their hardness of heart. (Mark 3:5)

He was greatly disturbed in spirit and deeply moved. (John 11:33)

Jesus [was] again greatly disturbed. (John 11:38)

When the Lord saw [the widow], he had compassion for her and said to her, "Do not weep." (Luke 7:13)

Looking up to heaven, he sighed. (Mark 7:34)

He sighed deeply in his spirit. (Mark 8:12)

In the pages of the Gospels we are not only shown Jesus' hands. We are also shown his tears. His heart. The deep places of his spirit. It is meaningful that these seemingly insignificant details were recorded. The Gospel writers felt it important not only to quote Jesus but also to record what he was like. He sighed. His eyes softened with compassion. He grieved. He wept. He was disturbed.

Our Jesus is compassionate. His heart leaps for people. His guts roll within him for people. Remember the widow in Nain (Luke 7:11-17)? As Jesus heads into Nain, a funeral procession is heading out. Jesus sees the mother of the dead man. He sees that she's a widow and "has compassion" on her (see verse 13). The Greek there literally means "his guts moved" for her. At the time this Gospel was written, guts were seen as the seat of all emotions. (We give the heart this distinction these days, but ask soul-sick people where they "feel" their sadness, and my guess is they feel it deep within their guts, not near the heart at all.) Whatever the case, the writer is making it clear that something deep within Jesus moved at the sight of this widow.

What ensues is an amazing story—amazing not only because Jesus raises the man from the dead but also because of the way Jesus' compassion for the woman seems to come across as the central point of the story. (Read through the story sometime and see if it doesn't seem written to emphasize Jesus' compassion rather than the raising of the son from the dead. For example, after being raised from the dead, the man sits up and speaks. What are his first words after coming back from the other side of the great gulf of death? We have no idea. The author doesn't bother to tell us. But the author *does* bother to mention that it was Jesus who picked the man up and handed him to his mother.)

It is significant that Jesus' manner and heart and compassion so struck the people of his day that the Gospel writers needed to describe that part of him while writing the Gospels. It is important that Jesus' great mercy and compassion are a part of the record of Scripture.

And it is significant that he is one acquainted with sorrow. So significant. He knows pain and suffering. When we are in moments of pain and grief, we can know that he understands and that he has compassion on us.

It changes everything to look at the flesh of God and see such mercy and tenderness and compassion.

COLLAPSE UPON HIM

So how do you respond to a Jesus who is gentle, whose hands comfort, whose heart is moved by those around him?

Jesus gives us a hint, "Come to me, all you that are weary and are carrying heavy burdens, and I will give you rest. Take my yoke upon you, and learn from me; for I am gentle and humble in heart, and you will find rest for your souls" (Matthew 11:28-29).

Jesus was gentle and humble in heart. He had mercy in his heart. And gentleness in his touch.

A man with such mercy and compassion is a place to go to for rest. For comfort. To collapse upon. I think it is significant that Jesus described his Spirit as a "Counselor" (John 15:26 RSV). Ever think about what that implies? It implies that we need one! It implies that the essence of his Spirit is compassionate and caring and understanding. We can weep with him. Collapse upon him. Know that he knows and feels and weeps alongside us.

This is the encouragement of Scripture: "We do not have a high priest who is unable to sympathize with our weaknesses, but we have one who in every respect has been tested as we are, yet without sin. Let us therefore approach the throne of grace with boldness, so that we may receive mercy and find grace to help in time of need" (Hebrews 4:15-16).

It wasn't until my junior year of college that I realized that collapsing upon Jesus was a valid expression of my faith. I had never read that verse from Hebrews and had always been very put together. Very dutiful. My understanding of the faith was *faithfulness*—doing what Jesus said. Doing the right thing. Jesus taught, I learned. And that was it.

That was it until the existential angst of life started catching up to me. My brother imprisoned, my mother having to leave a difficult marriage, my best friend in great emotional pain and all of

the ignored, filed-away emotions of twenty-one years of life starting to make their way to the surface of my heart.

I was a mess. Some days I'd wake up in my basement bedroom
and not be able to go into work or to class. I would just lie in bed
and cry. I was emotionally puking everywhere and was beginning
to be desperate. I had hardly ever cried before, yet all of a sudden
my heart and soul were leaking everywhere. Long-neglected feelings of inadequacy, loneliness and self-hatred seemed larger than
life, and the stuff of my faith (Jesus teaches, I learn) just wasn't
cutting it anymore.

I was desperate. Out of control.

It was then that I began to notice passages of Scripture that I
had never taken notice of before. The Psalms (the desperate
ones) finally made sense to me. Jesus' talk of healing started to
pique my interest. Stories of desperate people throwing themselves at Jesus, of outcasts running to him for solace, of sinners
bawling on his dirty feet began to resonate with my soul.

And I found, for the first time in my life, what it meant to collapse upon Jesus. To pray desperate prayers. Prayers laced with
cuss words and tears and groans. It was as if I had woken from a
long sleep and realized how thirsty I was. And what it meant to
receive living water. And how solid Jesus was. And how gentle. It
meant a lot to me then that Jesus was compassionate. Lowly in
heart. That he knew about tears and sighing. That he gladly gave
mercy to those who begged.

It was this humbling, seemingly embarrassing experience that
finally gave me a solid place to stand. Collapsing upon Jesus and
receiving his peace brought me to a place where I could offer real
mercy and peace to others, to be a minister in a world that was
desperately in need of some peace. And the same has continued
to be true over the years: the more I take my heavy loads to Jesus,
the more I am able to offer rest and peace to those around me.

ELUSIVE PEACE

Our world longs for peace. Everyone around us aches for a little rest, a little less heaviness in their souls and in the world around them. In our modern world, peace can seem a fiction, though. A pipe dream. An illusion.

No matter how many people hold up two fingers in that universal sign of peace, there continues to be war. No matter how many people take an interest in Eastern religions and the contemplative, spiritual, one-with-the-universe pursuit of inner peace, it seems we as a people grow more and more stressed and depressed every year.

Let's face it: peace eludes us. Isaiah's words are apt, "The way of peace they do not know" (Isaiah 59:8).

It has almost become too difficult to even understand the concept of peace. It is foreign. It is too large and beautiful to believe in. Many of us wind up pasting the word *peace* on much lesser experiences, claiming we've attained some kind of peace while—inside—we are most definitely not at rest. We are not peaceful.

To really understand peace, biblically, one has to become familiar with the word *shalom*. *Shalom* is the Hebrew word that we translate "peace." But it encompasses so much more than mere absence of conflict. True shalom is peace *between* people, *inside* people, *around* people. Shalom is comprehensive and lasting and deep.

Sounds nice. But is such a state even possible? Is it possible to have a true rest in our souls and between us as people and around us in creation? We don't even know the taste or smell or shape of true shalom. We sign treaties and create national parks and frequent our therapists. All to no avail. Peace eludes us.

But perhaps in Jesus there is a more sure route to peace than political protest and quiet meditation. In Jesus we have the hands that touch and calm, with mercy and grace and compassion. We have a Messiah who invites those who are heavy laden to come to him for rest.

We have the gift of his Spirit, which is a gift that this world does not know how to give. "The Counselor, the Holy Spirit, whom the Father will send in my name, he will teach you all things, and bring to your remembrance all that I have said to you. Peace I leave with you; my peace I give to you; not as the world gives do I give to you. Let not your hearts be troubled, neither let them be afraid" (John 14:26-27 RSV).

My peace I give to you, not as the world gives to you.

The world tries to give peace by urging us to avoid pain and conflict and suffering. We can find peace, so says the world, by sheltering ourselves, by isolating ourselves from the ugly parts of this planet. The more we're able to cocoon ourselves, the less pain and conflict we'll have and the more peace we'll feel. Just visit any gated community and you'll have a direct, visual parable of how our world gives peace.

But Jesus gives peace in a different way. Jesus never calls us to hide from an ugly, conflict-ridden world. He insists that we plunge into its darkest places. We are light in a dark place, salt in a decaying world, he says. Jesus calls us to lay our lives down for the people we bump into on this harsh planet. He calls us not to avoid pain but to embrace those in pain, to mourn with those who mourn. To draw near to pain. And weep for it. He calls us not to shun the lepers we may pass as we walk through our days but to embrace them.

But how can this aggressive, salt-and-light gospel life ever lead us to peace? Especially when we have so much pain and hurt and ugliness right in our very own souls? How could this ever lead to peace?

Through Jesus. That's how.

Before his death Jesus taught his disciples, "I have said this to you, so that in me you may have peace. In the world you face persecution. But take courage; I have conquered the world!" (John 16:33). In me you may have peace, he says. Peace won't come from placid, carefully controlled surroundings or suburban Christian cocoons. It comes from him. I find it interesting that after his resurrection Jesus' most common greeting for his disciples was "Peace be with you" (for example, John 20:19, 21, 26).

Paul tells us that Jesus himself "is our peace" (Ephesians 2:14). Our peace won't come from this world but from Jesus. Jesus the compassionate. Jesus the merciful. Jesus the gentle. The one who is acquainted with sorrow, who knows pain and knows how to comfort. The one who breathed his soul into the world at Pentecost as the great Counselor.

And because of gentle, compassionate, merciful Jesus, we don't have to pretend our own pains don't exist or run away from this world to safe cocoons. Because of him, we no longer have to shelter ourselves from the pains within us and around us. We can take it all to Jesus.

His is a peace that goes far beyond the understanding of this world because it is a peace that comes from him, not from circumstances. Our peace comes not from avoiding this painful world but from embracing it and taking all of the heaviness to him. His supply of mercy and patience and cleansing balm will not run out. His hands will never lose their gentle touch. But if that's all true, it begs an interesting question.

POTENTIALLY DANGEROUS QUESTION 7: *What would happen if we stopped pretending and collapsed upon Jesus instead?*

What if the church stopped the Grand Parade of Smiling Christians and instead found itself collapsing upon him in its need? What would that do to us? And to the world around us?

What if we stopped trying to hold it all together? What if we stopped medicating our inner pains with recreation and accomplishment and business? What if we ran and collapsed upon Jesus?

Perhaps we would find true shalom settling quietly into our souls. Not a sentimental, organ-induced ecstatic feeling. But a quiet knowledge of mercy. A true, slow peace.

Perhaps we could march forward as wounded healers, as beggars who have found bread, as peaceful sons and daughters. Perhaps our ministry wouldn't flow only from the reservoirs of our broken psyches and desire to grasp apostolic success but from souls that know rest.

Perhaps this world could look at the church and be intrigued by the inexplicable peace they see there. Instead of looking at the church and finding forced smiles and nicely tucked-in shirts and short, glib answers to the pains of life, perhaps the world would find a community of people who have the peace of Jesus within them. Perhaps they'd see lived-out testimonies of how freeing it is to admit the pains and struggles of life and take them to Jesus.

Where else is the world supposed to find peace? Where else will our heavy-laden neighbors hear about true peace, if not from those of us in the merciful embrace of Jesus? If not from those of us who have admitted our weariness and at last found rest for our souls?

The Gospel writers were careful to describe Jesus' compassion. They wanted us to know that in Jesus we have one who sheds tears for us, understands our pain and has a tender touch.

Their detailed descriptions of his mercy are an invitation.

———————————

May God be strong in our weakness.

May his ministry to our heaviness bring us rest. And may that true rest free us from our frenetic, worldly habit of running from conflict into cocoons of so-called peace.

Oh, for a day when we can stop hiding from this broken world and instead march calmly into it. With a gospel of peace.

May we see Jesus' gentle hands, real tears and deep sighs. May we see him as clearly as those two blind men and have the courage to cry out to him: Lord, have mercy.

Chapter Eight
They Struck His Head

Any careful study of themes found within the stage directions of the Gospels will eventually find itself in a very dark land. A land of negative, hateful, pride-laced responses to Jesus. A land of lies and insults and spitting and, ultimately, torture and murder.

Some of those we see around Jesus were astounded at his teaching. Others bowed to his authority. But there were some who had a very different, very angry response to Jesus.

If we are serious about taking what we can from the responses to Jesus recorded in the Gospels, we can't ignore this virtual flood of similar responses. We must make our way through them and see what we can learn of Jesus.

The Pharisees went and plotted to entrap him in what he said. (Matthew 22:15)

They said this to test him, so that they might have some charge to bring against him. (John 8:6)

All in the synagogue were filled with rage. (Luke 4:28)

People were saying, "He has gone out of his mind." (Mark 3:21)

The crowd answered, "You have a demon!" (John 7:20)

The Jews answered him, "Are we not right in saying that you are a Samaritan and have a demon?" (John 8:48)

The Jews said to him, "Now we know that you have a demon." (John 8:52)

Many of them were saying, "He has a demon and is out of his mind." (John 10:20)

They were filled with fury and discussed with one another what they might do to Jesus. (Luke 6:11)

They got up, drove him out of the town, and led him to the brow of the hill on which their town was built, so that they might hurl him off the cliff. (Luke 4:29)

The Jews were seeking all the more to kill him. (John 5:18)

The Pharisees went out and immediately conspired with the Herodians against him, how to destroy him. (Mark 3:6)

They kept looking for a way to kill him. (Mark 11:18)

The Pharisees went out and conspired against him, how to destroy him. (Matthew 12:14)

The chief priests, the scribes, and the leaders of the people kept looking for a way to kill him. (Luke 19:47)

They wanted to arrest him. (Matthew 21:46)

They conspired to arrest Jesus by stealth and kill him. (Matthew 26:4)

Some began to spit on him, to blindfold him, and to strike him. (Mark 14:65)

They struck his head with a reed, spat upon him. (Mark 15:19)

After mocking him, they stripped him. (Mark 15:20)

They kept heaping many other insults on him. (Luke 22:65)

All of them said, "Let him be crucified!" (Matthew 27:22)

Those who passed by derided him, shaking their heads. (Matthew 27:39)

The soldiers also mocked him. (Luke 23:36)

The chief priests also, along with the scribes and elders, were mocking him. (Matthew 27:41)

The bandits who were crucified with him also taunted him. (Matthew 27:44)

What are we to take from this river of angry verses? There's a definite theme to these responses, isn't there? It is worthy of our notice. It is significant.

Our contention has been that by looking at common responses to Jesus we can learn something of the man himself. Many worshiped him, which helps us see his divinity more clearly. Many marveled at his teachings, which clarifies just how profound and real his teachings were.

And many people mocked him. And spat upon him. And thought he was possessed. And sought to destroy him.

What do these responses clarify for us about Jesus? Surely these folks got it all wrong. Is there any real clarity that can come from looking at *these* responses to Jesus? Perhaps there is. Perhaps this overwhelming chorus of hatred and disdain actually tells us quite a bit about Jesus.

A SOLID MAN

For starters, we can know that Jesus was no people pleaser. He did not morph his personality or message or choices to stroke those around him. He was no respecter of persons, he did not cater to the powerful, he did not give people what they wanted. He was solid and prophetic and real. If his ways clashed with assumptions—fine. If his teaching caused a stir—oh, well. If his barbed truth speaking interrupted a nicely flowing party—okay. If his mercy and gentleness caused ire in the religious—so be it.

Jesus was not a man to be distracted by the whims of others or persuaded by what was popular. His purpose and truth and life were propelled and determined by his Father. And there would be no deviating. This chorus of human spitting and hatred and outrage is a testament to Jesus' prophetic nature.

He came as Light into a world that was fallen and dark. And those who live in darkness don't like lights so much—lights have a way of revealing. They have a way of chasing away lies and deceptions and false pride. Jesus was the Light and they hated him for it. They would have done anything to get rid of him. Their frantic attempts at destroying Jesus are a testament to the depth to which his razor-sharp message reached within them.

These black words also reveal Jesus' integrity. He was so far above reproach that his powerful enemies flung themselves about like desperate fish out of water trying to capture him. They, the keepers of the status quo, the holders of high positions, the determiners of law and custom and rule, could not get him.

Which of us could boast such a story? If I had enemies out to get me, they could. Quite easily. There's plenty of dirt and grime sticking to me. I have fallen and cursed and run away and struck the innocent and spread lies and . . . Let's just say they would have had no problem arresting me and convicting me before a jury of my close friends, let alone a jury of impartial peers.

And yet with Jesus this was not the case. The smartest men in town came together to try to trap him. But they had such a hard time getting any dirt to stick to Jesus that sworn enemies like the Herodians and Pharisees were forced to sit down together to pool resources.

All to no avail. They just couldn't get him. Even when they arrested him, their trials were a joke. They couldn't get their soldiers to pull off a successful arrest without falling down before Jesus, they couldn't get anyone to agree in their lies about Jesus during the trial. In the end it was an ugly, taped-together, fragile set of contradictory lies that convicted Jesus.

When they took this "evidence" before Pilate, he would have none of it. Jesus' innocence was just too glaring. He told them he wouldn't do it. He couldn't condemn this man who was so obviously pure and innocent. Pilate practically begged Jesus to defend himself and be done with this silly trial. But Jesus remained silent.

And only by stirring up an angry, senseless mob were the Pharisees able to get him finally sentenced to death. A kangaroo court of desperate men. Their feverish, repeated, silly attempts to entrap Jesus underline what purity and integrity Jesus had.

A STEADY, SURE MARCH

This chorus of negative responses highlights one more thing about Jesus—his utter, firm, persistent sacrificial nature. In his three years of ministry Jesus walked headlong toward death. At each awkward point of conflict with the Pharisees, at each run-in with his family, at each accusation slapped across his face, he could have hesitated, deviated, adjusted the plan to soften the blow to himself.

During his flogging, he could have stopped everything, unleashed his Creator power and destroyed all around him. Each time he was spat upon, he could have called down floods from heaven to wipe away those who would spit in the face of Yahweh enfleshed. When taunted upon the cross, when laughed at, when derided for not being able to save himself, he *could* have called legions of angels to his rescue.

The fact that Jesus elicited ire and hatred and lashings and insults from those around him tells us something deep about his longing to embrace death on a cross for us. Where each blow would have left most of us reeling and running for our lives and comfort and control, Jesus faced it all. He never let up, he never smoothed things over to slow the onslaught of pain and torture and death. He marched steadily into it.

Consider Gethsemane (Mark 14:32-52). Jesus becomes distressed and agitated. He is at the brink of the deepest pit of suffering and sacrifice imaginable—not just the momentary beating and spitting and taunting but also the colossal weight of ages of human sin slung around his neck, the recourse for every human evil and injustice ever committed slapped across his face, the penalty for every rape, child molestation, enslaved life, beaten minority being withdrawn from his very soul. And at the brink of this black hole of pain he pauses to pray.

In his agitation and distress he asks his friends to pray for him. He tells his closest friends that he is grieved—even to death. And asks for their support in this hour. He goes off and throws himself on the ground to pray, and in one great breath of prayer he asks that the cup of suffering would be taken from him and yet maintains his strong grip upon that same cup.

He spends time praying. A deep prayer that brings blood to his tears. His friends fail him and fall asleep. Three times. And in the end he wakes them. They are groggy, but he is filled with resolve. "Let us be going now, the time has come."

And he walks headlong into the slaps and pain and torture and unfathomable penalty for human sin. When the soldiers botch their arrest, he has to lead them through their task: "Who are you here looking for?" he cues them in their hesitation. "*I* am Jesus. I'm the one you're looking for. Come on now, you can do this, guys." And they fall back upon the ground (John 18:1-11). Even Jesus' enemies were falling apart.

But eventually they got it together, pulled along by the sure, sacrificial pace of this Jesus who fought through every blow and insult and pain to get to the point of being able to do his work on the cross.

THANK HIM

What do you do with one so prophetic, so full of integrity, so sacrificial? How should *we* respond to a Jesus who was fought with such anger and insult? That, my friends, is up to each one of us to answer.

But one thing is for sure. For those of us who stake our claim to life (for now and eternity) upon Jesus' sacrificial march, we should thank him. Among all else, let us thank him. For his resolve. For fighting his way through so many traps and temptations and insults without swaying from his course. All this was for us, after all. The sacrificial lamb walked straight into slaughter so that the blade would be used up before we ever got to that place of judgment.

Let us thank him for not stooping to please people but remaining steadfast in his purpose. Let us thank him for his purity and spotless integrity, without which he could not fulfill his purpose as the pure sheep readied for slaughter. Let us thank him that no series of blows and insults and nails and taunts could break his stride toward his set purpose.

We thank him because without that purpose each of us would be facing an eternity of death and pain and unfathomable, searing judgment.

But for many of us, giving thanks isn't quite so easy. Sure, I can say, "Thank you, Jesus," and even mostly mean it. But having a soul marked by praise and thanksgiving does not come so easily. Paul writes about "overflowing with thanksgiving" (Colossians 2:7 NIV), which isn't something I can say I have experienced a lot.

Thanksgiving has been difficult for me because so much of the well-being of my soul tends to depend upon my day-to-day circumstances. I am a slave to my own personal weather systems. If it's been a good week, I have an easier time feeling good about what Jesus has done for me on the cross. But if I am a little depressed or frustrated, my soul is anything but thankful. Sure, I can mouth the words of worship songs, but inside I am a cynical man.

Thanksgiving does not come so easily when I am living like a spoiled child, allowing the state of my soul to be governed by the finicky winds of my heart and circumstances. And it's tough to break out of this self-centeredness because of the rampant nature of cynicism in our culture. On top of all that, many modern worship songs, centered as they are upon me and my feelings about God, only tempt and buttress this self-centered posture of my heart.

How do we allow our souls to be wrapped around Jesus' work on the cross instead of our own frustrations and whims and thoughts of the day? How do we grow a deep, inner sense of thankfulness despite the cynicism that pervades our culture and daily leaks into our hearts?

In my own life two separate seasons have pegged my soul, more deeply than ever, to the solid work of Jesus on the cross.

The first season was a time òf clarity about my own sin. *How bad is my sin?* I wondered. I began to ask deep, honest questions about what I really believed about sin (sin is being naughty, doing little things that are fun but are for some reason outlawed by God) and began to study what Jesus said about sin (it's a dark land of deception, dizziness, slavery, spiritual suicide).

The more biblically I understood my own sin, the more brave my thanksgiving started to become. A clear theology of sin has been like water poured on the weak, dying plant of my thankfulness.[1]

The second season of life is a more recent one. I have been practicing the discipline of praying the Psalms.[2] And the thing about the Psalms is that they are extraordinarily honest ("O God, why do you cast us off forever?" Psalm 74:1) and yet anchored to God's goodness ("God my King is from of old, working salvation in the earth," verse 12).

My problem, I am finding, is that I allow my soul to be honest without anchoring it to the solid, historical work of God on my behalf in Jesus. So the psalms of my heart aren't exactly like the Psalms in Scripture. Mine spin off into self-centered bunny trails of anger or apathy or pride, without ever being brought back to the truth of God's goodness.

The more I allow the Psalms to instruct my prayer, the more I find thanksgiving coming naturally from my heart. In our cynical, psychiatric, self-worshiping culture the Psalms sound foreign, but they help me become more free in my natural thankfulness. When I pray the Psalms, I feel less enslaved by my own petty inhibitions and ever-changing whims.

In general my heart is accustomed to the rhythms of entitlement and cynicism. They are dark, sick dances. But they are familiar. Thanksgiving feels like some foreign dance. The beat is different, the steps are strange. My heart feels awkward, shy. Facing the reality of sin and learning the honest but rooted nature of the Psalms is like giving my heart dance lessons.

ELUSIVE ME

We all long to live in our own skin. As humans, that is, we all have the desire to really be individuals. To be ourselves. Unique and free. And yet so often we settle for groupthink or a herd mentality or something like that. We define ourselves by being a part of a group, happily roaming through life as a We.

Now, there is a great truth (and even miracle) in this *We* that is right and appropriate. We all long to belong. To have a family, a home, a people. We were created for such belonging. And the kingdom of God is the only true, lasting place to find it. And for many of us (this skinny, shy introvert included), that is a real miracle. Entering into community is a sign of the amazing work of God.

But there still remains this longing to be ourselves. To be Me. An I. It's a desire that's wired into us, I believe. And I think it's often out of this desire that we resort to clothing or hobbies or achievements to set ourselves apart as unique. But looking different and even being acknowledged and applauded by others doesn't quite satisfy this desire to be a Me. To really live in our skin. To stand before all of creation, before God himself, as an accepted, individual, unique part of the world. To have God look us in the eyes—not just give a look in the general direction of humanity but give a look directly in our own eyes. And to feel his acceptance.

And this is where the great, sacrificial nature of Jesus comes in. For his work on the cross, such a bloody, painful, searing, courageous work drives us each to a very personal place.

In 2004 Mel Gibson released a movie called *The Passion of the Christ*. This movie was a feature-length film focusing exclusively on the suffering Jesus endured on the way to the cross. It was graphic and violent and detailed. In the long run the movie drew a mix of responses, but when it first came out, a very interesting thing happened in theaters across the country: silence. Yes, silence. When the movie ended and the credits started rolling, many theaters remained encased in silence. No one moved.

Most wouldn't even turn their heads to talk with their friends. Not every theater audience responded this way, of course, but many did.

Based on my own experience and the stories others told me, I believe that silence illustrates just how personal and how deep our response to Jesus' sacrificial nature really is. Why were the theaters so often silent at the end of the movie? Why did it take so long for folks to turn and say anything to their neighbor? Precisely because Jesus' passion drives us each to a very personal place. And thus it should be.

As Søren Kierkegaard put it, "Every call from God is always addressed to one person, the single individual. Precisely in this lies the difficulty and the examination, that the one who is called must stand alone, walk alone, alone with God."[3]

We must remember, of course, that Jesus' death on the cross makes real reconciliation and community possible. I thank God for how his work makes it possible for me to relate with others more freely than ever. But Jesus' work on the cross also drives us all to stand in our own skin. It frees the I within us to be itself, to stand alone from all else, looking God in the eyes and seeing his incredible love displayed for us on that cross. And this personal, intimate, vulnerable place to stand fulfills something within us, this great desire to be a Me.

While God longs to have a people, and we are thus called into the community of the kingdom (in great contrast to the shallow individuality of the culture we live in), God also longs for us to stand freely in our own skin and look him in the eyes. Again, as Kierkegaard puts it so well, "God desires to have *I's,* for God desires to be loved."[4] God and me at table are sat down.

This desire in us to be individuals, and the desire in God to relate with individuals, brings up an important question to let loose in our lives.

POTENTIALLY DANGEROUS QUESTION 8: *Would Jesus have done it just for you?*

I know, I know! This is an incredibly trite question. But if we can get beyond its triteness and cheesy familiarity, a wonderful kernel lies waiting in the center of this question. A kernel of truth that I believe calls to deep places within each of us.

What if only you and Jesus lived in this universe? What if only two sets of feet plodded upon this earth, yours and his? What if your brokenness and sin were the only brokenness and sin to be found within the galaxy? Would he do it? Knowing it would save your eternity, would he still walk through all that pain and torture just for you?

When you see a crucifix, is it personal? When you stare at this sacrificial Jesus, are his eyes wanting to meet yours? Or do they blankly stare at humanity in general? It is that stare alone that can help us stand as free individuals in our own skin.

Only through him can any of us really be a Me.

Oh, Jesus, help us let go of our self-centered grip on reality. Help us stare so deeply and intently upon your suffering and torture and steadfast posture that we have stir within us a desire to stand before you alone. As we will stand on that day when we see you again.

Help us to shake off this vague, general sense of your historical gesture toward all humanity and embrace instead your intense, dramatic, personal effort for us.

Help us stand before God and all of creation and know who we are because of you. Our cynical world and petty fetishes want to pull us in very different directions. So we pray. And beg.

Book Five
The Call of Jesus

When Jesus entered a town, he usually stirred up quite a flurry of motion. Sick people rushed to him in throngs, healthy people ran off in different directions to look for their sick friends, and some people reacted to him with strange, drastic actions. Actions like risking their reputations, flinging aside valuable family heirlooms and walking away from careers.

What was behind all this motion? And what do these drastic responses teach us about our own responses to Jesus?

Chapter Nine
They Brought to Him All the Sick

Read through the black verses of the Gospels and you'll inevitably be struck by how many mosh pits you see.

Well, not mosh pits exactly, but close enough. Something akin to a rock concert, anyway—huge crowds jostling, pressing in to get closer to the "star," Jesus. But it wasn't an autograph these folks were after.

> They brought to him all the sick, those who were afflicted with various diseases and pains, demoniacs, epileptics, and paralytics. (Matthew 4:24)

> That evening they brought to him many who were possessed with demons. (Matthew 8:16)

> All in the crowd were trying to touch him, for power came out from him. (Luke 6:19)

> After the people of that place recognized him, they sent word throughout the region and brought all who were sick to him. (Matthew 14:35)

> People were bringing even infants to him that he might touch them. (Luke 18:15)

All who had diseases pressed upon him to touch him. (Mark 3:10)

She had heard about Jesus, and came up behind him in the crowd and touched his cloak, for she said, "If I but touch his clothes, I will be made well." (Mark 5:27-28)

Immediately the people recognized him, and ran about the whole neighborhood and began to bring sick people on their pallets to any place where they heard he was. (Mark 6:54-55 RSV)

Wherever he went, into villages or cities or farms, they laid the sick in the marketplaces, and begged him that they might touch even the fringe of his cloak. (Mark 6:56)

Reading all these verses in a row brings into greater focus how many people unabashedly sought Jesus out for healing. Again and again, whether asking him face to face for healing, laying the sick strategically where he might pass by or sneaking up from behind, people longed for his healing touch.

Though his authority led many to kneel silently before him, though his divinity led many to lift up praises at his mere presence, Jesus was by no means unapproachable or untouchable. In fact, as we see in these verses, many people found themselves going to extremes just to touch him.

But what do these desperate, mosh-pit crowds teach us about Jesus?

BASHING HOLES IN ROOFS

First we need to recognize that not only did the sick seek him out unabashedly but also friends and relatives of the sick went out of their way to get their sick friends and this powerful Jesus together. The Gospels make it clear that upon word of Jesus' entrance into a town many folks would drop whatever they were doing, run to their diseased, oppressed friends and carry them around town, sweating, running, yelling out to anyone who would listen, "Where is he? Where is he? Is he still here?"

The Gospel records also make it clear that no attention was given to Jesus' schedule, no space was politely afforded him. There was no standing on the outskirts of the crowd politely waiting your turn, no quietly raised arms. Folks ran and pushed and scrambled and shoved—all for a touch. Just consider the four guys who took their paralyzed friend to find Jesus (Mark 2:1-12).

Their story probably began days earlier. You see, it's pretty safe to assume that these same guys had tried to get their friend healed by Jesus the first time Jesus was in Capernaum. "That evening, at sundown, they brought to him all who were sick or possessed with demons. And the whole city was gathered around the door. And he cured many who were sick with various diseases, and cast out many demons" (Mark 1:32-34).

I imagine these four guys had brought their friend that first night too. It was a sabbath, and news was spreading of this Jesus who had healed a man with an unclean spirit at the synagogue. So as soon as the sun set (sabbath officially ending), the whole town showed up at the house to see if it were true. People brought to Jesus all the people who were sick and possessed. The whole city was gathered about the door!

I can just see these four friends jetting out of their houses at sunset, breathlessly gathering up their friend, running through the streets, assuring their confused friend that this man could indeed heal him. Can you imagine the paralytic daring to believe it were possible? Could I really walk again? Can you imagine the joy of the friends? Maybe we'll finally be able to be a basketball team together! Okay, maybe not basketball. But you get the picture. Their friend was going to be healed!

But that first night didn't work out so well. Maybe they were at the back of the crowd. Maybe there were just too many people. Jesus didn't heal everyone—we know that the next morning the whole town was looking for him with more folks to be healed. But Jesus went away, moving on to preach in other towns.

Just try to imagine the deep soul deflation in those four friends and in the paralytic. So close to real, healing power. But alas, no. It just wasn't meant to be.

With this context from Mark 1, we can see what an understatement we have in the first verse of the next chapter: "When [Jesus] returned to Capernaum after some days, it was reported that he was at home" (Mark 2:1). You bet it was! And the whole town comes around again. The four friends run and get their friend, and as they run through the streets, perhaps the paralytic is daring to hope again (hoping is such a dangerous thing for the heart!). And perhaps the four friends are making plans for the next intramural basketball season. But when they find the house, they are too late. Again.

Jesus was inside teaching. And the house was full. There was no way to get to Jesus—even the doorway was packed. The paralytic must have sighed, resigning himself again to a life of shame and powerlessness.

But his friends couldn't handle it. Their friend's need was so present, so palpable, so sad. And Jesus' power was so close—just inside those four walls! They couldn't just walk away. Should they set their friend down and wait out the crowds? (Jesus would have to come out eventually.) Should they send one of their group in to see what was going on? Should they simply give up and come back later?

Somewhere in the brainstorming process—somewhere desperate and beautiful and clear—one of them suggested the ridiculous. I know—let's climb on the roof and bash a hole above Jesus and drop him on Jesus!

And somewhere even more desperate and beautiful and clear, they all agreed.

They dove headlong into the ridiculous, climbing to the top of the house and beginning to bash their hands against the dried mud and straw until, bit by bit, pieces began to give way below and a hole started to open up.

Oh, the shocked stares that must have come up at them through the first small hole! But stares or no stares, they pounded away until a gaping hole large enough to lower their friend through was formed. And lower him they did—right into the midst of the room. Anything to get their friend closer to this powerful Jesus. Anything.

And who can blame them for their lack of politeness? Who can look down on them for acting so brashly and suddenly? What else could they do? To be around so much need and so much power— they just had to get the two together. There was no choice or deliberation. There was no calm bowing to social customs. They were in the presence of power! Power like none other they had ever experienced.

And what do you do when you see such power? You leap. You run. You get up off your couch because there's finally a place to take your own need and the needs of those dearest to you.

There is a great ache in humanity: to get need close to power. To get the oppressed to one who can liberate. To get sickness to one who can heal. To get thirst to water. Perhaps one of the most profound human desires that we'll ever experience is the desire to get need close to power.

The chorus of folks pushing to be near Jesus or running with their friends to Jesus shows us that Jesus was a rescuer, a liberator, a healer. His touch had power. We can't explain away the desperate frenzy of those pushing in toward him by assuming that they were rude people. We can't dismiss the story of the four friends and the paralytic by assuming that they were overly aggressive or that they were extroverts. No. They were human. And to be human is to be drawn to power. To be human is to know (at some deep level) exactly what to do when power comes to town.

From the distance of two thousand years, we can calmly speculate about Jesus' power. But for those who were there, who had him walk right into their dusty towns, there was no speculation. His power was present, obvious, palpable. And being near such power led them to bring their need to him.

Their aggressiveness and insistence are a testimony to just how powerful Jesus was. His touch changed people. That was a power the world had never seen in a man.

BRINGING ALL THE SICK TO HIM

So what do we do with this power? What do we do when we see the Gospels proclaim with such clarity that Jesus' touch is powerful?

Well, we should run after Jesus! He encouraged us to be persistent in our prayers, to keep after him. So let us throw our need at his power. Let us beg for a touch from him. Let us believe that such a touch would bring fruit.

Let us run around town to a sick friend's house and pick him up off his couch of pain and carry him, breathlessly, to Jesus. There's sickness everywhere, after all. Physical sickness is all around us, even in our country. And the deeper sicknesses—loneliness, addiction, shame, suicidal thoughts, rape, isolation, bitterness . . . and the overarching weight of sin—are at pandemic proportions.

If Jesus really is so powerful, why aren't we more regular and persistent in laying our own needs before him? If his touch contains such power, why aren't we, like those we see in the pages of the Gospels, running about town to bring all in need closer to his powerful touch?

Because we no longer believe that Jesus' touch carries power. We just don't see him like those in his own day clearly saw him.

Instead we grow accustomed to illness (physical and spiritual), and we cope and deal. We farm out the spiritually ill to professionals who can rarely heal but who will sedate the problem enough to keep it off our conscience. I'm not suggesting there's no need for doctors and professional counselors and even medication. I'm just suggesting we've lost all fight as a church when it comes to carrying our needy friends to Jesus.

Now few of us would claim out loud that Jesus has no power today, since that would be such obviously bad theology. But it's what we believe, I think. We silently swallow the assumptions of our scientific age until we find ourselves ignorant of the clear gospel teaching that Jesus has all power.

In the summer of 1999 I was confronted with my own working theology of a powerless Jesus.

My wife, Wendy, and I were leading a small team of college students on a mission trip in Mexico's Yucatán. We were partnering with small Presbyterian churches in tiny, remote villages. Toward the middle of the summer, we were invited to stay for a couple of weeks in Teya, the smallest village we had yet come across. Teya was hard to get to, but when we arrived, we were welcomed by a dozen faithful members of the church in town.

We moved in with these families, sharing their humble, dirt-floored huts with them. We strung up our hammocks and settled in for a couple of weeks of ministry in the church.

A few days into our trip, Wendy got sick. She woke early one morning in pain. She had little energy. And a fever. When our team got ready for the day, we left Wendy to rest and drink water, a combination that usually does wonders. We were gone all day. During that day, she lay in her hammock, growing weaker, not able to keep any water in. By the time we came back for dinner, she lay miserable and quiet in her hammock. She looked terrible.

We were concerned. As her husband and the leader of the team, I wanted to do whatever I could to help her get better. We talked about taking her to the nearest doctor—too far to go that evening. I consulted my handy So-You're-Leading-a-Group-into-the-Jungles-of-the-Yucatán medical handbook—and could only give her some medicine to slow down the diarrhea so maybe she could hold in a little water.

And then I was out of tricks. I had nothing else in my med kit that might help. There was nothing else to do. We were rushed at dinner because of a large event that evening that we were leading and had been planning for all week. So we grudgingly left, telling ourselves that Wendy would be okay until we got back.

When we got back, she was sitting up, laughing, happily eating a large bowl of soup. We were stunned. And thrilled. Wendy was beaming and told us what had happened.

While we were gone, José and Nancy, our host papa and mama, came into the room. They were a humble, joyful couple. José worked in the fields outside Teya, Nancy took care of their family and small home. When they walked in, José told Wendy (with simple words that even Wendy with her limited Spanish could understand) that Jesus was going to heal her.

He knelt down next to her hammock and lifted his deeply tanned arms to heaven. And praised. Afterward Wendy could only describe his worship time through tears. The simplest, most beautiful praise she had ever witnessed. Then he placed his hands on her head and, kissing her forehead, said, "Estás sano," simply assuring her she was healed.

Wendy immediately felt a tingle in her feet. As José calmly told his wife that Wendy was healed and would need some soup, Wendy felt the tingle start to move up her legs. When the tingle reached her stomach, the nausea left. When it got to her head, she felt the fever dissipate. She was healed.

Jesus had healed her.

I had done everything I knew how to do, except pray. In faith. There's nothing wrong with medicine, of course. And doctors and their knowledge are a real gift from God, I believe. But there is something wrong—I realized that breathless night standing next to my wife in a dirt-floored hut in Teya—with not believing in the power of Jesus. There's something wrong with not even thinking about seeking his healing touch for my wife whose pain was so obvious and pressing.

Jesus is powerful. And that means something. I don't believe the Gospel writers recorded episodes of people flocking to Jesus with their sickness and oppression and desperate need for no reason. They were recording and clarifying for all time the amazing power that Jesus has. Which brings us to an important question to consider. It's a question we need to deal with.

POTENTIALLY DANGEROUS QUESTION 9: *Does Jesus still have the power to heal?*

Is there still power (both physical and spiritual) in his touch? Or has he become impotent? Has he become a bystander not willing or able to heal those who would press in to him? History tells us otherwise. And my wife tells me otherwise.

Now, I know that there are many who would argue for a dispensational understanding of Jesus' healing. I hear the reasoning that Jesus was granted healing power in those days in order to testify to his holiness as he first brought his gospel upon the earth.

But I also read about healing in the early church. And I hear Paul assure me that "the power at work within us is able to accomplish abundantly far more than all we can ask or imagine" (Ephesians 3:20).

I also saw a miraculous healing that day in a small Mayan village.

Does Jesus still have the power to heal? This is a jagged little question. It has the potential to help us rip off the sensible blindfold of our scientific age and throw our lives back into the land of faith. A realm where we believe (dare I suggest it?) in the invisible. In the miraculous. A place where we rest our faith in powerful Jesus himself rather than in our placid religion and the limited scope of power we've seen evidenced in our churches up until today.

It's a question that has the potential to dig into the comfortably settled soil of our hearts and overturn the pained, oppressed status quo we've steadily grown used to over time. Maybe we've just grown so accustomed to our pains that we don't really want to be healed. I certainly don't assume that we all want to be healed. Jesus had to ask the blind men, "What do you want me to do for you?" (Matthew 20:32). He had to ask the man stranded at the pool, "Do you want to be made well?" (John 5:6). So I have to ask myself if I really want to be healed too. Do I want to touch him, to receive something from him right now?

It's a question that makes us examine ourselves: Am I sick? Where am I sick? Are there places of pain and hurt and addiction and shame that I've grown dull to over time? That I've pushed down and covered up as a survival strategy? These questions make us look in the mirror and just might lead us to our knees, to a place of desperately pleading for a healing touch.

Does Jesus still have the power to heal?

A potentially dangerous question. Potentially dangerous because it threatens our predictable, superficial religion. And potentially dangerous because asking it could lead to a Holy Spirit-invoked season of evangelistic fervor like our churches today have only read about.

ELUSIVE EVANGELISTIC FERVOR

Seasons of ingathering in the church, of a real zeal for inviting people to enter the kingdom, are dependent upon many things. Chief of these is the will of God as expressed in his Holy Spirit. Revival can't really be humanly scheduled and planned and conducted. Not real revival. These seasons are under the sovereign control and direction of only one—God.

Even so, it is also true that a healthier church is more apt to be faithfully and regularly inviting people into God's kingdom, regardless of the fruits or outcomes of the invitations. It's this faithful evangelistic fervor that so many pastors and leaders would love to see more of in their congregations, regardless of the numerical outcomes. An evangelistic church is a healthy church. But maintaining an evangelistically charged church is difficult.

It's difficult because such a church must be willing to enter into pain and mourning. We're talking about the lost here, and their lives are often twisted into sick, pained dances governed by The Liar and by their own fallen wills. Really coming alongside such people will inevitably lead to mourning. And mourning is messy and hard and inefficient. Though Jesus assures us that those who mourn are blessed, it is also true that mourning is patently un-American.

It's difficult to maintain a healthy evangelistic fervor because our cynical, prideful age loudly proclaims a relativistic, broken mantra that makes our simple belief in hell and heaven and the surety of eternal judgment seem silly and old-fashioned. Why would we internally long to invite others into the kingdom if nothing real or lasting or eternal is really hanging in the balance?

It's difficult to maintain an evangelistically charged church because, as Jesus illustrated again and again in his teachings and life and death, pursuing the lost is difficult and costly. It requires sacrifice and patience and persistence and faith and selflessness and recklessness. And that's a difficult path to walk.

After all, how many times have we ramped up for huge seeker events, spending amazing amounts of money on fliers, a band and great food, only to see few if any non-Christians actually come to the event?

True evangelistic fervor is just mighty difficult to produce or sustain. After all, how many roaring, tear-jerking sermons about evangelism have we sat through with shame and conviction and breathless agreement, waiting anxiously to be released from the service so we can go and tell the world about Jesus, only to find the message and the conviction and breathless agreement fade quickly from our minds and hearts and hands and feet?

How we love the idea of having a "heart for the lost." How we'd love to see our congregations have more "evangelistic fervor." And how helpless we are to put that passion within actual hearts.

The truth is, evangelistic fervor is not some quantity we can put in a can and label and distribute. It has to grow from within. Mourning the brokenness of the world is one key part of the soil that such fervor can grow within. A wide-eyed theology of judgment and eternity is another key part of this soil. But only when such mourning and conviction are combined with a deep and specific understanding of the power of Jesus will an evangelistic fervor find root within our hearts. To see and know and be convinced of his power—his true, undeniable, still-with-us-to-this-day power—is to find a heart for the lost growing within us.

Let me put it as plainly as I can: Knowing a lost friend makes you sad. Knowing a lost friend and an utterly powerful Savior makes you get up off your couch and run.

May we heed the testimony of all those in the Gospels who ran to Jesus. May we know Jesus in all his power. And may we find our hearts beating wildly within us.

We need to stop stressing over the how-to's of evangelism: How do we create a seeker service? How do we invite a friend to study Jesus without risking our friendship? How do we make a flier that will appeal to the lost? To be honest I myself am quite tempted to digress into such questions even now as I finish this chapter. They are important questions in many ways. And asking them is so invigorating, so sexy, so . . . postmodern.

But such questions often just lead us down either of two very unhelpful paths. The first path dead-ends quickly, leading us to a place where we freeze entirely, not daring to proceed with any evangelistic efforts. (We don't want to get it "wrong," after all, and offend our lost neighbors.) The second path is another type of dead-end, but it's a dead-end of the subtle sort. We allow these how-to questions to enter us into lots of "evangelistic activity" that involves sitting in front of a computer or baking cookies or making trips to Kinko's rather than actual human contact, actually carrying our flesh-and-blood friends to Jesus.

Instead of spending all our time asking these how-to questions, let's start by feeling the need around us and being duly reminded of Jesus' power. When we truly feel our friends' need and truly accept the reality of Jesus' power, all of the stressful how-to's of evangelism fade in significance. Just ask the four friends of the paralytic.

They deeply felt their friend's need. (They didn't struggle with any relativistic nonsense that would convince them that being a paralytic and begging on the streets wasn't so bad.) And they had clearly seen the power of Jesus. (Not being duped by a modern age that sneers at faith and assures us so-called believers that what we follow is void of any real power.)

So, "how-to" get their friend to Jesus? Well that question wasn't very tough at all. That was the easy part. I'd even venture a guess that that was the fun part!

Once that longing desperation is within you, once you've felt the pressing need of your friends and seen the present power of Jesus, you find a way. Trust me, you find a way! We can be very creative when we need to be.

Just ask those four friends.

———————

Oh, for a desperate church. For a church that reaches out the hands of its own sicknesses again and again toward the touch of Jesus.

Oh for a faith that leans persistently toward Jesus, content to touch merely the fringe of his garment, rather than unblinkingly farming our needs out to the world or slowly burying our need in a silent, jaded, politely façaded posture of perpetual pain.

Oh, for a church that has faith in the power of Jesus.

A church that loses its seriousness and simply runs—gathering up friends to bring them toward Jesus. Bashing through whatever walls or roofs or obstacles are keeping our friends from having a chance to be within a hand's reach of Jesus.

Oh, for a church that is desperate enough to become creative.

Oh, that we would know what to do when power comes to town.

Chapter Ten
They Left Their Nets

By now we've seen a lot about Jesus. Studying the black verses of the Gospels has been fruitful. Scripture is so rich that even these seemingly boring verses are dripping with clarity and theology and truth.

By looking at the responses of those around him, we see Jesus' holiness and divinity, his brilliance and authority, his mercy and love, and his very real power. But there's one final collection of black verses we need to consider before I feel comfortable putting down this study. This set of verses is the hardest one to quantify. There's not a lot of short verses that are easy to scan. But the more I hang out in the pages of the Gospels, the more I see this theme. It's apparent. Plainly obvious.

It seems that interacting with Jesus caused some folks to do drastic things. Drastic, almost epic, beautiful things. They . . . abandoned themselves to Jesus. It's hard to put it any other way. Consider a few examples.

Immediately they left their nets and followed him. (Matthew 4:20)

Immediately they left the boat and their father, and followed him. (Matthew 4:22)

He got up and followed him. (Matthew 9:9)

Mary took a pound of costly perfume made of pure nard, anointed Jesus' feet, and wiped them with her hair. (John 12:3)

She stood behind him at his feet, weeping, and began to bathe his feet with her tears and to dry them with her hair. Then she continued kissing his feet and anointing them with the ointment. (Luke 7:38)

Zacchaeus stood there and said to the Lord, "Look, half of my possessions, Lord, I will give to the poor; and if I have defrauded anyone of anything, I will pay back four times as much." (Luke 19:8)

There are some obvious differences in these verses. The first few are about men leaving their vocations, walking off the job to follow Jesus. The next couple are about women who plunder their dowries, pouring perhaps their only savings upon Jesus. And then we see a rich man giving away much of his wealth (if not most of it—depending on how many people he'd defrauded).

But the similarities are striking. In each case we see a drastic response to Jesus. They are all going a bit overboard, you could say. There doesn't seem to be anything careful or measured about their responses to Jesus. They are epic and unencumbered and bold and intense.

But what do these drastic responses show us about Jesus?

LEAVING NETS BEHIND

Let's consider some of these threshold moments more closely.

We see these two brothers, Simon and Andrew, running their fishing company. It's morning and they've been fishing all night.

They are tired, their hands are busy working the nets to mend them for their next outing. This is all the life they've ever known. They are Galileans through and through. They are fishermen. Not just their vocation but their self-perceptions are tied up in this moment of working their nets. And yet, at a word from Jesus, they drop the nets. They drop their lakeside lifestyle and start walking with Jesus.

For James and John it's the same. Except we are told they are with their father, Zebedee, in the boat. The men of the family are mending the nets together—something they had done together hundreds of times and would presumably continue to do thousands more times over the course of their years. Theirs is a family business. A trade. A tradition. And yet at a word from Jesus, James and John drop the nets and walk away from their vocation, their boat and their father.

Matthew's job is different. Matthew is a man of money. A leader of tax collectors who could have risen to his post only by being successful as a tax collector himself. In other words, he was good at extortion, was incredibly motivated by money and had a practiced callousness to the pleas and cries of those who had no more money to spare for the Romans. And one day Jesus is walking along and sees him sitting in his tax booth. At a word, Matthew leaves it all.

The women's stories are different. For them it isn't a bold walk away from the comforts of their vocation. Instead they literally pour out their only personal wealth on Jesus. These jars and their precious ointments were rare and expensive and were likely something they were saving for harder times. And yet at merely seeing this Messiah carpenter, this gentle man of the people, both "spend" it all on Jesus. And both pour out their tears as well, in tender moments of washing his feet. All this in public. At great risk to themselves and their reputations.

And then there's Zacchaeus. Like Matthew, but shorter. When Jesus comes to town, Zacchaeus has to climb a tree to see him. When Jesus stops underneath the tree and invites himself to Zacchaeus's house for dinner, the crowd grumbles, but something clicks inside Zaccheus. Something about Jesus' invitation makes him pledge away much, if not most, of his money to the poor and oppressed.

Now, perhaps a better understanding of the cultural context would clear up some of these seemingly rash actions. Maybe Zebedee would be happy to see his sons go off with a rabbi. Perhaps Jesus had known these fishermen for quite some time and had gone over with them what a life of following him would look like. Maybe they were tired of fishing. Perhaps Matthew was a friend of Jesus' already. Perhaps wasting whole jars of nard was commonplace. Perhaps a bath of tears was normal in their culture. Perhaps Zacchaeus hadn't defrauded many people in his vocation as a tax collector. Perhaps.

But what is crystal clear in the Gospel telling of these stories is an undeniable sense of awe and epic abandonment. When Jesus is in the room, treasures and lives and careers have a way of getting flung away. Social customs and etiquette and decorum have a way of dissolving into nothing. This is the clear testimony of these verses.

There is a beauty in Jesus that calls forth reckless abandon.

Jesus is beautiful. And at a word from him, thick-bearded men with calloused, practiced hands drop their familiar nets. At merely seeing him from behind, a woman invites herself into a house she has no right to be in and halts a dinner party with her weeping. At the mere mention of getting to host Jesus in his house, a chief tax collector's tight grip on money is loosened to nothing.

What was it in Jesus that elicited such epic abandonment? His holiness, his brilliant teachings, his palpable authority? Maybe it was his power or gentleness or divine scent? Or maybe, when you add up all these aspects, you get a striking, compelling . . . beautiful man. A man who calls forth to something deep within, with a call that makes all other calls or impulses or duties fade away.

Deep calls to deep. And human ambition and control and fear fell from human hands. Witness the beauty of this carpenter, and a long life of measured, careful steps might just get traded in for skipping along with him into the great unknown.

Jesus had this effect on people.

And he still does.

ABANDON ALL FOR HIM

What do you do with such a man, such a Messiah? A carpenter with such obvious holiness and brilliance and authority and power and mercy and divinity and love and beauty?

You abandon all for him. This clear vision of Jesus takes over your heart and soul and body and you find yourself living differently. Throughout history it's been those who seem really impressed by Jesus, really taken with his holiness and power and beauty, who end up living lives of reckless, joyful abandon for him.

Remember Paul on the road to Damascus? After a tongue-in-cheek "bragging" about how much he had in life before meeting Jesus, Paul proclaims, "Whatever gains I had, these I have come to regard as loss because of Christ. More than that, I regard everything as loss because of the surpassing value of knowing Christ Jesus my Lord. For his sake I have suffered the loss of all things, and I regard them as rubbish, in order that I may gain Christ" (Philippians 3:7-8). Paul was taken with this looming figure, Jesus. And he lived a life abandoned to Jesus, in joy.

Remember Francesco di Bernadone? Francesco was a young,

uppity, gregarious, self-indulgent Italian boy. But then he saw Jesus. And became preoccupied with him and *in love* with him. And so he laid aside his privilege and family business and military pursuits of glory. St. Francis, we call him. A man who has become well known as a singer, a man of joy and peace. His reckless, drastic life for Jesus left him as a poet and singer and a man remembered for his laughter.

Remember that middle-aged geography teacher in India who laid aside the comforts of the cloistered life in response to Jesus? Mother Teresa, we call her. A woman whose peace and joy and contentment were always as striking as the destitution she chose to work within. Journalists would always ask her about her ministry, the poverty, the hard conditions, and she almost always responded by talking about Jesus. Her dear, sweet Jesus. Mother Teresa was taken by Jesus, betrothed to him, preoccupied with him. And her life and energy and comfort were poured out upon him in the distressing disguise of the poor.

Not everyone is called to leave his or her vocation, of course. Our reckless abandonment should look as varied and unique as we are: leaving a fishing company, cracking open your prized alabaster jar of nard, walking into synagogues to preach about Jesus, caring for the poor in the name of Jesus rather than caring for our bank accounts in the name of leisure . . .

The call is always from Jesus and is as varied as we are. But the response is the thing. When we see Jesus clearly, our own cares melt away. And we will do whatever he says.

And thus is the history of the church at its best: simple folks laying it all on the line for Jesus. And finding deep contentment. Think of your own heroes of the faith. What is it that's so appealing in them? Isn't it how they spent their lives? And found contentment and joy and peace in the process?

Isn't that what we all long for? To be unencumbered? To respond to Jesus with everything we have? To abandon ourselves to him every single morning? When I see the reckless abandonment described in the pages of the Gospels, and find it echoed in those I most look up to, it makes me ask some serious questions about my own life, my own abandonment, my own journey as a disciple and lover of Jesus.

POTENTIALLY DANGEROUS QUESTION 10: *When I see Jesus clearly, what do I most want to do?*

In those moments when I consider Jesus and who he is and what he was like and what he did for me, are there any crazy, reckless thoughts that waft through my consciousness? I think that there probably are and that they are important, for they come from the deepest, bravest parts of my being.

But we usually ignore these whispers of abandonment, dismissing them as reckless and foolish. And we move on with the staccato march of our controlled lives.

But we're missing the chance to live from our souls. Sure, our *minds* and *hearts* get involved: yelling thoughts and feelings about how such ill-advised abandonment would certainly leave us. So we heed their loud complaints.

But our souls rarely yell. They whisper. They long to live and to respond to this beautiful Jesus who calls to our deepest parts.

ELUSIVE PURPOSE

But what will happen to us if we get swept up in Jesus' beauty and end up losing our life as we know it?

Well, according to Jesus, we will finally find life: "Those who want to save their life will lose it, and those who lose their life for my sake, and for the sake of the gospel, will save it. For what will it profit them to gain the whole world and forfeit their life?" (Mark 8:35-36).

Jesus said this several times to his disciples. His repetition shows how central this teaching is and how difficult it is to grasp. He painted word pictures too:

> The kingdom of heaven is like treasure hidden in a field, which someone found and hid; then in his joy he goes and sells all that he has and buys that field.
>
> Again, the kingdom of heaven is like a merchant in search of fine pearls; on finding one pearl of great value, he went and sold all that he had and bought it. (Matthew 13:44-46)

What beautiful, clear pictures of spending all we have, abandoning all we have in exchange for something that ultimately leaves us satisfied and joyful! It's Jesus' promise: our lives, only in submission and abandonment to him, will be saved, be abundant, have true meaning and purpose.

It makes complete sense, and yet we still try to "save" our lives. We just don't want to lose life in order to gain it. I know I have spent many seasons of my young life trying to save it, trying to maintain some sense of control and steadiness and safety. I see beautiful Jesus and hear his call to abandonment . . . and hesitate.

For me it's safety. Or predictable isolation. There's this cabin in the woods, you see. It's a place I long for when Jesus' simple words invite me to lose my life. His call sounds alive and thrilling—and scary. So my instinct is to retreat to my cabin of safety.

The cabin doesn't exist, of course. It's an icon in my head. A fantasy image of what really "saving my life" on my own would look like. It's a nice cabin. Small, snug. Far away from crowds and cities and relationships. There's a satellite dish and a basketball hoop and a dog. And no one else. Shelves of books line every wall. And if I were able to go there, I would be safe and moderately occupied and free from pain or dangerous relationships or ringing phones or needy people knocking at the door.

This cabin haunts me. It tempts me. It tells me that it would be wise to save my life a little bit, to make sure I'm carving out plenty of safe space between me and this dark world around me. It tells me I'll be satisfied there in that isolation. It's a temptation from The Liar himself. It tells me that Jesus is dangerous, that if I listen to his call, I will end up hurt, unprotected, surrounded by people. And for this skinny introvert, that's a weighty argument.

This iconic cabin and its siren song took a hit a couple years ago. I was on a trip with my wife, and some friends had arranged for us to stay with a retired couple from their church one night of the trip.

As we followed the directions to their house, we began to realize we weren't heading into the nearest city but into the beautiful hills several miles outside of town. After miles and miles of small roads that wound through leafless aspen trees, all shrouded in snow, we came around a bend and saw it. The cabin.

I am not kidding you. We were staying with a retired couple who were living in something that looked an awful lot like my "safe place." Walls of split logs, vaulted ceilings, books everywhere, a spectacular view and—yup—a satellite dish. There was no basketball hoop, but there *was* a hot tub, which made up the difference just fine.

That night I sat in the hot tub with the owner of the cabin. I sat there staring at him. He was living my dream life. Or something close to it. My skin grew wrinkly and my glasses fogged up as I sat there staring face to face, so it seemed, with my deepest temptations. And it didn't look too bad! I stared at him and dreamed about what it would be like to have his life.

Then the owner starting asking me questions about *my* life, and that's when it happened. This man, who was living a parable of what most tempts me not to abandon all for Jesus, started becoming intrigued by my life. He was curious about being a campus missionary, he was intrigued that I spent my summers in the city, learning from the poor. He kept asking for more and more stories. Then he got quiet. And wistful.

With a soft voice and a faraway look in his eyes, he began sharing with me what he had done with his life, how thoughtlessly he had marched into a career and settled for the toys it afforded him. His tired voice dripped with regret as he told me of the pains of retirement. Of the boredom, of looking back at a life that had accomplished nothing lasting, of having stood for nothing and made no great stand for anything.

And as the steam sifted above the water and rose up into the dark night sky, I realized that he was sitting there and longing for my life. This man who had everything The Liar tempted me with was dissatisfied. Terribly dissatisfied. My iconic cabin in the woods tarnished that night. Its siren call hasn't been the same since.

And I am a little freer to hear Jesus' repeating call to lose my life in order to really save it.

No matter how strongly we're each tempted to carefully save our lives, when it comes right down to it, we all want our lives to make sense, to have stood for something. Martin Luther King Jr. argued that if you haven't found something worth dying for, you aren't fit to live. That's a bold claim. A chilling conclusion.

But I think that in our more silent moments, when we pause from the frenetic crush of life, many of us do have a sense of the passing of time. We realize that our days on this planet are limited and being spent quickly. It's in these moments that we realize we have only one shot at this, only one life to spend here. And we want it to count.

We all long for purpose, fulfillment, satisfaction. Life isn't really worth living without that. If we are all given just one life to spend, then we are going to make it count. But in the end everything we try seems to leave us wanting. Everything, that is, until we meet Jesus. And look into his beauty.

As it would seem from the Gospels, abandoning all to Jesus really works. It's the only way to spend our life well.

In the end we can but smile at beautiful Jesus and admit that saving our life is possible only in him. That true contentment and purpose and meaning and life are found only in him. That if we try to grab hold of life on our own, to try to *save* our life, we will ultimately *lose* real life and contentment and purpose and meaning.

Ultimately, life itself is elusive. And as we abandon our lives for Jesus, we find true life growing within us.

Oh, let us gaze into his eyes. Let us stand before this humble carpenter and let his beauty knock down our defenses. And our pride. And control and shame and hesitancy. And let us run with him a wild race of truth and beauty and grace. Let us pour out our most treasured prizes upon him, only him.

Let us abandon all for him.

Let us no longer be couch-sitting Christians who are known more for our dogma than for the actions of our hands and feet. Let us become people of the Way. Jesus followers. The word Christian implies religion and dogma and sedentary intellectual assent to a belief system. Enough of that!

Let us throw off this heavy blanket of cultural Christianity and relearn how to run. How to repent. How to lose our lives instead of always trying to save them. How to be used by God. How to change this world.

Let us relearn how to stare, how to worship, how to study, how to kneel, how to touch, how to trust. Jesus is so rich. So full. So utterly captivating and beautiful and worth everything we have. He is all.

Help us stand before your beauty with open eyes, Jesus. And help us respond from the bravest parts of our souls.

Conclusion
Breakfast with Jesus

There is so much more to say. These pages are so incomplete, so lacking, so bare. But of course, mere pages can never do the trick.

As the apostle John (the wonderfully gifted and divinely inspired author) put it at the end of his own telling of the life of Jesus, "Now Jesus did many other signs in the presence of his disciples, which are not written in this book" (John 20:30).

An interesting confession, isn't it? There's just no way to get it all in, he admits. Jesus is too full, too rich, too divine, too beautiful to get it all in. And yet John (even after admitting how much he's having to leave out) can't let his pen rest yet. He has to record one more story. He just can't help it. And if you can fit only one more in, he reasons, it has to be this one.

You can find this one story at the end of his Gospel (John 21). It's the story of Peter and Jesus having breakfast at one of their favorite spots, the shore of the Sea of Galilee.

Now, it's important to note that, leading up to this breakfast, Peter has been acting differently. He just hasn't been himself since Calvary.

A REALLY STRONG MAN, SORT OF

Before Calvary, Peter always came across as a man of strength and oaths and aggression. Or weakness and fear and pettiness. Kind of depended on when you caught him. Of all the disciples, Peter defined the extreme ends of the spectrum of human strength and human weakness.

Consider the moments leading up to Calvary. It's Peter who bravely stands up to Jesus' admission that one of the disciples will betray him. "Though all become deserters because of you, I will never desert you" (Matthew 26:33). What bravado! What pluck! He actually argues with Jesus over this point and ends with a defiant "Even though I must die with you, I will not deny you" (verse 35).

And the next moment Peter can't even stay awake for Jesus. Three times Jesus asks him and the other disciples to please stay awake and pray for him (the first time Jesus has ever explicitly asked for personal support from his disciples), and yet Peter falls asleep. Again and again and again. What weakness and pettiness and hypocrisy.

But when the soldiers come, it's Peter who pulls out a sword and starts fighting! Strong Peter is back.

But then all the disciples flee, including Peter.

But in the end Peter *does* follow at a distance. "Going inside, he sat with the guards in order to see how this would end" (Matthew 26:58). Maybe he's planning an escape? Maybe he still has his sword with him? Whatever the case, we know it took bravery to sit in among those guards.

But then a servant girl recognizes him as a follower of Jesus and he swears he doesn't know what she's talking about. Another servant girl recognizes him, and "again he denied it with an oath, 'I do not know the man' " (Matthew 26:72). And when the crowd gets in on the questioning, "he began to curse, and he swore an oath, 'I do not know the man!' " (verse 74).

After that last denial, the cock crows.

Peter weeps. And is dropped from the narrative.

The trials happen. The cross happens. Saturday goes by. And Peter is nowhere to be seen in the narrative of any of the Gospels. And we're left to wonder: which Peter will surface on the other side of the cross? Strong Peter or weak Peter?

A MAN ENAMORED

As it turns out, neither. A different Peter.

Consider what we see from Peter once the narrative picks him up again: Peter runs to the tomb after hearing that Jesus was risen. (Sure, he's a slow runner, but as soon as he puffs his way there, he runs right past timid John!) Peter jumps into the lake and swims to Jesus. (Once he recognizes that it's Jesus, he puts on his clothes and dives in. He can't even wait for the boat to sail in!) Peter hauls in the nets of fish by himself. (Jesus had asked all the disciples to help, but it's Peter who pushes them all aside and does it himself.)

This does seem like a different Peter, doesn't it? He's acting a little silly for a grown man. Running? Jumping into the water to swim to Jesus? I would argue that he's almost acting like a man in love.

Have you ever been around people who are falling in love? They're all helpful and energetic and giddy. They never walk toward their beloved casually (Peter ran to the tomb), often do silly things when their beloved is around (Peter dove into the water and swam to shore) and usually have lots of energy and helpfulness flowing from them (Here—I'll get those fish!).

And that's the Peter we're shown after the cross. I am not suggesting any sort of romantic love, of course. But Peter *is* acting differently. Before the resurrection, he was an intense man, rocking back and forth between strength and weakness. A tight-fisted man of purpose and oaths and intensity.

But then Easter happens. And Peter is a different man. Something new seems to be happening inside him.

And then Jesus has breakfast with him on the shores of the same sea where they had first met. And after breakfast Jesus has a question for Peter. Only one question.

I probably would have asked Peter if he was going to deny me again. Or if he was feeling drowsy again. (I can be pretty sarcastic.) If I were Jesus and were about to hand Peter the authority to start and lead my church on earth, I would want to know if he was going to be more stable, more strong, more consistent. But no. Jesus has only one question for Peter. A simple one: *Do you love me?*

Do you love me?

He asks three times. And three times Peter says that he does. And three times Jesus calls him to "feed his sheep." Peter's new role and authority, Jesus asserts, do not rest on his strength and consistency and oaths but on his love for Jesus.

This is the story John just had to fit in. A story that illustrates what Easter did to Peter and how crucial Peter's affection was in the eyes of Jesus. Jesus wanted Peter to remember what it was really all about. And I think he did.

In his first epistle it's Peter who writes, "Although you have not seen him, you love him" (1 Peter 1:8) and "Love one another deeply from the heart" (verse 22) and "Finally, all of you, have unity of spirit, sympathy, love for one another, a tender heart, and a humble mind" (3:8). Tender heart? Humble mind? Peter is definitely a changed man!

Imagine what it did to folks who knew Peter his whole life to receive a letter from him addressed to "Beloved" (for example, see 1 Peter 4:12) or that instructed them to greet each other with a "kiss of love" (5:14).

FIXING OUR EYES ON JESUS

Based on his letters, we can see that Peter remained a man of love. Preoccupied with this Jesus who had died for him. It would seem that Peter remembered that last breakfast and what Jesus had asked him on those shores.

And John wants us to remember too. I think that's why he just had to squeeze in this one last story. Because when it comes right down to it, that question (Do you love me?) is the most important question. Period. Not will we be strong enough? Not will we get it all right? But do we love Jesus? Are we taken with him? Are we captivated by him? Do we *love* him?

That's really what it all comes down to. When we're just practicing religion (even this religion called Christianity), it's all about our strengths and weaknesses. Will we do the right thing? Will we get it all right? Are we dutiful? Are we reading enough, studying enough, pleasing God? Or are we weak and failing?

But Easter does away with religion. It's not about human strength and weakness anymore. It's about having breakfast with Jesus. It's about the person of Jesus and his life and death and resurrection. It's about being preoccupied with him, staring at him. And falling in love with what we see there.

It's about becoming simpletons.

It's about seeing Jesus clearly, in all of his holiness and brilliance and authority and power and mercy and divinity and sacrificial nature and beauty. It's about taking the Gospels seriously and seeking in their pages the true image of Jesus that has been handed down to us.

And it's about being changed by that clear image. It's about finding the seemingly elusive blessings of life growing from within. Blessings like unity and thanksgiving, wisdom and humility, peace and evangelistic fervor. Blessings that can't be corralled or forced with human strength.

Blessings that come only from within as we become Jesus saturated. Blessings we see in full force in Jesus' early church. A church that was careful to remain preoccupied with Jesus. A church that guarded its image of Jesus well.

Seeing the flesh of God clearly changes people, regardless of what century we are talking about. This is the story of the church. This is the story of Paul and Peter and John. And it could be our story as well.

When we are focused upon Jesus, it's not the religion game anymore. It's about folks like Peter being transformed. I think that's why John had to sneak this last story in. And after recording this beautiful, paradigmatic, powerful interaction between Peter and Jesus, the Gospel writer is spent. He ends with the words that are on my own pen today, "But there are also many other things that Jesus did; if every one of them were written down, I suppose that the world itself could not contain the books that would be written" (John 21:25).

And so it is. He is beyond all of us.

Notes

Chapter 2: Blurry Jesus

[1]George Orwell, "Politics and the English Language," in *The Norton Reader: An Anthology of Expository Prose*, 6th ed. (New York: W. W. Norton, 1984), p. 392.

[2]Ibid.

[3]Ibid.

[4]Ibid., p. 395.

[5]Søren Kierkegaard, *Practice in Christianity*, trans. Howard V. Hong and Edna H. Hong (1848; Princeton, N.J.: Princeton University Press, 1991), p. 128.

[6]Martyn Lloyd-Jones, *Revival* (Wheaton, Ill.: Crossway, 1987), p. 45.

Chapter 8: They Struck His Head

[1]For a more full discussion of this theological and spiritual journey, see Don Everts, *The Smell of Sin: and the fresh air of grace* (Downers Grove, Ill.: InterVarsity Press, 2003).

[2]Reading Eugene Peterson's *Working the Angles: The Shape of Pastoral Integrity* (Grand Rapids: Eerdmans, 1987) has plunged me into this discipline.

[3]Søren Kierkegaard, *Søren Kierkegaard's Journals and Papers*, vol. 1, ed. and trans. Howard V. Hong and Edna H. Hong, as quoted in Søren Kierkegaard, *Provocations: Spiritual Writings of Kierkegaard*, ed. Charles E. Moore (Farmington, Penn.: Plough, 1999), p. 315.

[4]Søren Kierkegaard, *Søren Kierkegaard's Journals and Papers*, vol. 4, ed. and trans. Howard V. Hong and Edna H. Hong, as quoted in Søren Kierkegaard, *Provocations: Spiritual Writings of Kierkegaard*, ed. Charles E. Moore (Farmington, Penn.: Plough, 1999), p. 317.

Questions and Applications

CHAPTER 1: FIXING OUR EYES ON JESUS

Questions for Reflection or Discussion

FIXED EYES

If someone were to look closely at you (or your church or fellowship), would that person be able to conclude that you knew nothing but Jesus? How would you evaluate the overall focus of the Christian books you read, sermons you listen to and songs you sing?

JESUS AND US

Do you think often about the person of Jesus? How much time have you spent in the Gospels in the last month? How would you say you feel about Jesus these days? What's your favorite Jesus story from the Gospels?

HIS LIFE AND HIS DEATH

What do you think about the idea that we need to look at Jesus' life, not just his death? Do you agree that it is a danger to ignore the life Jesus lived? How could you focus more on his life?

Applications for Further Thought or Action

1. Read a Gospel in one sitting. Really. Find a quiet spot and a spare two hours, get a copy of one of the Gospels (Mark is the

shortest) that doesn't have a lot of commentary in the margins and enjoy yourself. Simply take in the story. Stare at Jesus as he marches through the pages. What new things do you notice about Jesus? What strikes you about the story when you read it all in one sitting?

2. If you're in a group, have everyone get quiet and comfortable and close their eyes. Then have someone read some Gospel stories from Eugene Peterson's wonderful contemporary version of the Bible, *The Message*. Afterward, share about what it was like to sit and listen as well as about what you thought of Jesus in the story. What did the story reveal about God?

3. Using various art supplies, create a picture of what Jesus looks like to you. You could use old magazines and cut out pictures or words that fit your picture of Jesus, then glue all of these together on a page. Share with others what you created and why. If you're in a group that meets regularly, feel free to add to your collages over time as you learn more about Jesus.

CHAPTER 2: BLURRY JESUS

Questions for Reflection or Discussion

LIES

What are some of the most obvious lies about Jesus that are popular these days? Which are most dangerous, in your opinion? Do you agree that looking back to the Gospels is a good way for the church to combat these lies?

HOME BLINDNESS

Have you ever experienced home blindness with something in your house? Do you think it's possible to suffer from home blindness with Jesus and his gospel? Have you ever experienced that or seen that?

What do you think about George Orwell's conclusions about modern language? Do you notice a leaning toward "sophisticated" words about Jesus and the faith in your own life? In the lives of your Christian friends? How do you think this trend has affected the church?

Applications for Further Thought or Action

1. Play a game of Christian Taboo. Gather a group and, together, agree upon a list of words that are too "spiritual sounding" or "sophisticated" to make sense to the average non-Christian. (For example, words like *salvation, redemption, forgiveness, sin, repentance.*) Then take ten minutes to write an answer to the following question without using any of the off-limits words: *What is the significance of the cross in your life?* After ten minutes, read to each other what you've written. Afterward, debrief what it was like to answer the question without using the off-limits words.

2. Take a common Gospel story (try one of Jesus' more popular parables, such as the prodigal son or the good Samaritan, or a common healing or miracle) and rewrite the story using a different voice to help you see it from a different perspective. For example, write using a Southern dialect or the language of a six year old.

3. Get a copy of Calvin Miller's *The Singer: A Classic Retelling of Cosmic Conflict* (Downers Grove, Ill.: InterVarsity Press, 1975) and read a few chapters, discussing with others what this mythical retelling of the gospel did to bring new clarity to your image of Jesus.

CHAPTER 3: THEY WERE SEIZED BY AMAZEMENT

Questions for Reflection or Discussion

HOLY JESUS

When was the last time Jesus surprised you or made you grin? Which Gospel stories make you feel like you've "seen strange things"? Would you describe yourself as proud of Jesus? Enthralled with him?

OUR FOCUS

In your faith and spirituality, what do you most often "stare at," or find yourself focusing on? How central is Jesus to your personal prayer and study? To your church's services? Think about the last time you shared about your faith with a nonbeliever; how central was Jesus to what you shared? How many times did you mention him?

UNITY AMONG BELIEVERS

What word would you use to describe your most common feelings about or reactions to other Christians or churches in your town? What were you doing the last time you felt unified with other believers? Do you think unity is a real possibility or just pie in the sky?

Applications for Further Thought or Action

1. Read John 17 (Jesus' prayer for the unity of his followers) and then pray with him for the same things in your town. Drive around town, stopping in front of five to ten churches and pray for their congregations. Give thanks for their presence and for God's work in their community. As you go on this prayer tour, ask Jesus to speak to you about how unity will be made possible in your town.

2. Look up a few of the blue-collar verses listed at the beginning of this chapter and find out the context. What was it that made people so shocked and amazed? Do those things amaze you? What would it take to amaze you today? Make a list of the traits of Jesus that impress you. Carry this list with you and see how long the list can grow to become over the next month.

3. Read chapter 5, "Profile: What I Would Have Noticed," in Philip Yancey's book *The Jesus I Never Knew* (Grand Rapids, Mich.: Zondervan, 1995). What new things do you notice about the life and ways of Jesus after reading this chapter?

CHAPTER 4: THEY WORSHIPED HIM

Questions for Reflection or Discussion

LIES ABOUT JESUS
Why would The Liar be interested in dulling us to the full divinity of Jesus? How does he specifically go about that these days?

WORSHIP IN EVERYDAY LIFE
When was the last time you yelled (a pleasant yell) about how cool or great someone or something was? Are *loud* and *joyful* the best words to describe how you (or your church) are in worship? If you were to pick two adjectives to describe your worship, what would they be?

THE PRESENCE OF GOD
Do you think God lives in you and around you? Do you *feel* like God lives in you and around you?

Applications for Further Thought or Action

1. This week, go to a worship service at a church that worships in a different style than that of your home church. Maybe take a friend with you. Feel free to observe, but at some point try to take off your Whoa-This-Is-All-New-and-Intriguing-to-Watch-and-Observe glasses (which we all put on when in a new church) and try to participate.

2. Try practicing the presence of God, reminding yourself throughout your normal day about God's real presence in you and around you. For example, you could wear a necklace or bracelet or pin that you'll see often during the day. Or set your watch to go off every hour. Anything that will jog your mind so you can remind yourself of God's presence. See what it does to be mindful, more regularly, of God's presence.

3. Read a psalm every morning for a week. But don't just read it, read it out loud. And not just softly out loud, really out *loud*. Proclaim the truths that you find there as if they are true and are words worthy of being proclaimed on this earth at this time. See what it does to practice the spiritual discipline of voice, actually giving voice to your words about God. Maybe start where the disciples did on the way to Jerusalem—with Psalm 118.

CHAPTER 5: THEY BECAME SILENT

Questions for Reflection or Discussion

JESUS' TEACHINGS

Why do you think so many people around Jesus were amazed by his teachings? What's your favorite Whoa-Jesus-

Is-Really-Brilliant moment when you experienced a seemingly upside-down teaching turning out to be rock-hard reality? Do you think Jesus' teachings are still true today? For every situation?

SEEKING WISDOM

Are there ways you (or your church) settle for simply reading Jesus' teachings rather than submitting to them? Who do you know who strikes you as deeply wise? How did he or she get so wise?

THE LIAR

Why do you think the enemy is particularly interested in our losing sight of the brilliance of Jesus? What are some of the ways you think he goes about blurring this part of Jesus in our eyes?

Applications for Further Thought or Action

1. Read Luke 6 (on your own or in a group) and list all of the teachings from it that seem absurd or upside down. Then choose one from your list and give Jesus a month to really teach you about the truth of that teaching. Ask him what it would mean to try out that teaching for a month, to be good soil for that seed.

2. For a whole month, try ending every time in Scripture (whether personal devotional reading or a group Bible study) with this question: "What would my life look like if I really believed this?" See what the habit of asking this question does to you.

3. Choose a section of Jesus' teaching from the Sermon on the Mount (Matthew 5—7) and ask a non-Christian friend to study it with you. Find out what your friend thinks about Jesus'

teachings. As you study these sections, reflect on which passages you disagree with. Pray honestly about these passages with Jesus.

CHAPTER 6: THEY FELL DOWN BEFORE HIM

Questions for Reflection or Discussion

THE FEAR OF THE LORD

When was a moment in the last year when you really sensed the authority of God? What do you think about the fear of the Lord? Does it have a place in the New Testament Christian church?

THE LIAR

Why would the enemy be particularly interested in us losing sight of the authority of Jesus? Is it difficult these days to remember and acknowledge the authority of Jesus? What do you think makes it so difficult?

HUMILITY

How would you describe humility? What do you think of the descriptions and images about humility in this chapter? What kind of power do you think there is in humility? What do you think would be the biggest change in your town if your church started to grow into a truly humble community?

Applications for Further Thought or Action

1. For the next week, kneel on the ground every time you pray or worship. Experiment with the posture, see if you can incorporate it into your spirituality and faith. Pay attention to the effect this posture has on the content of your prayers and worship.

2. Find a section of Scripture that speaks of God's authority, and read it out loud. (Try the creation accounts in Genesis, many of the Psalms, the ending of Job or many parts of Revelation.) If you're in a small group, have someone read the section out loud while everyone else has their eyes closed. Read through it two times. Slowly. See what God brings up.

3. Spend your next quiet time outside where you will be confronted with God's creation. (Even just looking up at the sky can help.) Contemplate how big and powerful he is as you spend time with Jesus. Pray with your eyes open, looking at the immensity of his creation.

CHAPTER 7: HE TOUCHED HER HAND

Questions for Reflection or Discussion

THE LIAR

Why would The Liar want us to lose sight of the mercy of Jesus? In what ways does our view of Jesus' mercy get blurred or sidetracked? Why do *you* think the Gospel writers recorded these seemingly small details (the touch of a hand, a sigh, tears)?

OUR HEAVINESS

What does it feel like to see this side of Jesus? Is it uncomfortable? Comforting? When was the last time you felt weary or heavy laden? Do you believe it's really possible to find rest for your soul?

PEACE TODAY

Do you see peace when you look around your community? What people do you see who seem weary and heavy laden? What would it do to your community if folks in your church were finding real rest for their souls and were free to embrace the stressed people around them? What would this peace of Jesus affect first in your community?

Applications for Further Thought or Action

1. Get alone in a place where you won't be interrupted for a whole hour. Use the time and space to take an inventory of your soul. Where do you feel weary? What is a heavy burden for you? Take all of that to Jesus and beg for comfort and mercy. See what happens.

2. Choose one of the verses from the second list in this chapter. Look up the context and read through the whole story, trying to picture it happening. Maybe draw a picture of the scene, trying to capture the emotion on Jesus' face, the sigh coming from his soul, the tears coming from his eyes or the compassionate moving of his guts. Or write a poem about the scene that helps get at Jesus' compassion. Put what you've created in a place you'll see it regularly over the next month. See what it does to your own posture before God to be mindful of his compassion.

3. Watch the 1986 documentary *Mother Teresa* made by Ann and Jeanette Petrie. How powerful can compassion and mercy be? What aspects of Jesus do you see reflected in Mother Teresa?

CHAPTER 8: THEY STRUCK HIS HEAD

Questions for Reflection or Discussion

THANKFULNESS

Is it generally easy or hard for you to feel thankful for Jesus' suffering and work on the cross? Does your internal weather change quite a bit? Do you feel swayed by it? What do you

make of the claims that our culture is cynical? Do you think
that affects our thankfulness?

BEING A ME

What do you think about Kierkegaard's thoughts about the individual? How do you fit that in with the call to community?
Do you agree that all humans really desire to be a Me? Do you
feel that desire? When was the last time the cross felt real to
you? What happened to make you feel it that way?

THE LIAR

Why would the enemy want to dull us to Jesus' true sacrificial
nature? How does he go about nudging us away from a clear
view of this? How could something so drastic and clear, like the
passion of Jesus, ever be rendered less powerful?

Applications for Further Thought or Action

1. Watch a movie or part of a movie that depicts Jesus' passion
   and death on the cross, or reread the verses from this chapter
   a few times. Ask Jesus to heal you of the subtle ways you may
   have become dulled to his sacrificial nature.

2. Stare in a mirror for thirty minutes straight. Look in your own
   eyes. Perhaps hold a small cross in one hand during this time,
   but really try to be in your own skin. If it gets awkward (it just
   may), try to not look away and don't give up! Ask Jesus to speak
   to you through the awkwardness, to show you what it feels like
   to be in your own skin. Ask him what he thinks about you.

3. Skip church one week. (I recognize that in general this is an
   unhealthy habit, but for a one-week experiment in worship, I
   think it's worth it.) Hold a one- to two-hour church service by
   yourself, in your own home. Do normal church stuff—sing,
   pray, recite the Lord's Prayer, whatever. And do it out loud as

you would in church. Maybe have Jesus' cross be the theme of the service. See what it's like to be in your own skin before God. Pray that God would help you be a Me with him.

CHAPTER 9: THEY BROUGHT TO HIM ALL THE SICK

Questions for Reflection or Discussion

THE LIAR

Why do you suppose the enemy is interested in blurring our view of the power of Jesus' touch? How does the enemy most often go about blurring that aspect of Jesus from our view these days?

SICKNESS IN ME

As you consider your own heart and soul and mind and body, what needs do *you* have? Do you believe Jesus wants to heal you? Do you believe he can still heal people these days? What would it look like to desperately pursue Jesus for a touch?

SICKNESS AROUND ME

What makes you mourn? What kinds of needy people are there in your town? How many of them are you close to? Think of one of those folks—do you really think a touch from Jesus could meet his or her needs? Have you ever felt programmed into doing evangelism? How did it go? How did it feel? If Jesus came to your town today (in body, just like he did in Capernaum), who would you run to get first?

Applications for Further Thought or Action

1. Write a journal entry from the perspective of the paralytic after the day recorded in Mark 2. Step by step, go through the

day "remembering" what you might have felt at each point of the story. After writing his journals, spend a few minutes considering what your deepest need, your "paralysis," is these days. Take a few moments to imagine what would it be like to no longer suffer from it. Take all of the questions and feelings this exercise might bring up for you to Jesus.

2. Read chapter one, "What's Our Box?" in Rick Richardson's *Evangelism Outside the Box* (Downers Grove, Ill.: InterVarsity Press, 2000). Process the questions at the end of the chapter for yourself or for your church or fellowship.

3. Ask Jesus if there's someone he wants you to aerobically and lovingly bring to him. Take the next week to more attentively than usual listen for an answer. Pay attention to any people God may bring to mind. If God does bring someone to mind, consider inviting them to do a few sessions of Scripture study with you. *Meeting God in the Flesh: 8 Discussions for the Curious and Skeptical* (Downers Grove, Ill.: InterVarsity Press, 2005) is written for just such occasions.

CHAPTER 10: THEY LEFT THEIR NETS

Questions for Reflection or Discussion

LEAVING OUR NETS

When was a time when you abandoned all to Jesus? What was it like? Do you think it's possible for more of life to feel that way? What might it look like to "lose your life" for Jesus in your current context?

THE LIAR

How do you think The Liar feels about how you're spending

your life? What do you think The Liar wants you to do with your life? What are the subtle (or not so subtle) ways he tries to tempt you, personally? What's your "cabin in the woods"?

ELUSIVE PURPOSE

Do you feel like you're "spending" your one life well? Are you satisfied? Fulfilled? What do you think of Jesus' claim that we save our life by losing it?

Applications for Further Thought or Action

1. Ask Jesus what it would mean to lose your life for him. Spend at least one hour quietly listening. Follow this prayer time by filling out a time line of your life thus far. While filling it out, ask Jesus to speak to you about your life and the different seasons of your life. Maybe ask him what season is coming next.

2. Ask an honest friend to have coffee with you and share with him or her what these verses of abandonment bring up in you, what questions they make you ask. Ask your friend for counsel or any honest observations about your life.

3. If you've read the earlier chapters, go back and reread the chapter with the Gospel verses that most impacted your view of Jesus. Maybe do one of the suggested applications from that chapter that you haven't done yet.

ALSO BY DON EVERTS

Meeting God in the Flesh

Can we really meet God in the flesh? This discussion guide for
groups investigating God looks at the simple, seemingly insignificant actions and reactions of people who encountered Jesus. A
companion to Don Everts's book *God in the Flesh;* eight sessions.

Jesus with Dirty Feet

Unencumbered by religious language, Don Everts presents an
easy-to-read, upbeat and unapologetic introduction to Jesus and
shows why making a decision about him is important.

Jesus with Dirty Feet Discussion Guide

In this discussion guide, a companion to the book *Jesus with
Dirty Feet,* Don Everts and Douglas Scott offer ten sessions of
candid inquiries into who Jesus was, what he was like and
whether or not it matters.

The Smell of Sin

In poetic, narrative theology, Don Everts calls us to reclaim an
understanding of the seriousness of sin (which Jesus taught so
clearly) and to celebrate the difference that this knowledge can
make in our everyday lives.

Available from InterVarsity Press
www.ivpress.com